CW00822356

PO
Gulf
COLT
Firestone
AAW
NESTE OY

RSCHE 917

ACKNOWLEDGEMENTS

Thanks to:

Doctor Ferdinand Piëch
Hans Mezger
Peter Falk
Helmut Flegl
John Horsman
Vic Elford
Derek Bell
George Follmer
Roger Penske
Reinhold Joest
Ermanno Cuoghi
Jo Ramirez
Peter Davies
Josef Hoppen
Achim Stroth
Alvin Springer
Klaus Reichert
Audi AG Automobil-Presse
The Ludvigsen Library
Peter Schmitz
Bob Carlsen
Bettie Jo and Leonard Turner

Unless otherwise credited
the photographs are from:
LAT Photographic
Standard House
Bonhill Street
London EC2A 4DA

IAN BAMSEY
BILL OURSLER

PORSCHE

917
KURZ · LANGHECK · SPYDER

THE ULTIMATE WEAPON

26
20
30
24
25

A **FOULIS** Motoring Book

First published 1987

Published by:
Haynes Publishing Group, Sparkford, Near Yeovil, Somerset BA22 7JJ, England.

Haynes Publications Inc.
861 Lawrence Drive, Newbury Park, California 91320 USA.

Produced for G. T. Foulis & Co. Ltd. by
RACECAR ENGINEERING
(Specialist Publications)
18 North Street, Chiselborough,
Somerset TA14 6TH, England

British Library Cataloguing in Publication Data.

Bamsey, Ian
Porsche 917: the ultimate weapon.
1. Porsche 917 automobile—History
I. Title
629.2'28 TL215.P75

ISBN 0-85429-605-0

Printed in England by:
Adams & Sons (Printers) Ltd, Hereford.

Title page, in colou
Rodriguez and th
Porsche 917: a Gr
driver in a Great
here pictured at S
in 1970. That yea
Rodriguez was
partnered by
Kinnunen who we
on to find success
a 917/10 spyder c
the Interseries tra
(inset).

Previous page, in colour —
Start of the 1970
1000 km. Porsche
917 versus Ferrar
512 was a one-sid
contest until Ferr
caught up Porsch
head start on
development. The
917s of Siffert an
Rodriguez are sid
by-side (Siffert
the outside) chase
by similar cars fr
Gesipa (no. 30),
AAW and Salzbu
while Elford's 91
lags behind the
Bonnier Team
Chevrolet-Lola T
and the Ferrari f
takes to the othe
side of the road.

eaf, in colour—
Variations on a me. Rodrigiuez' 17 is pictured at Monza in 1970 aring a standard Kurz tail (lower otograph) and at Daytona in 1971 rting the revised JWA tail with al aerofoil. The er was regularly from Le Mans 1970 onwards.

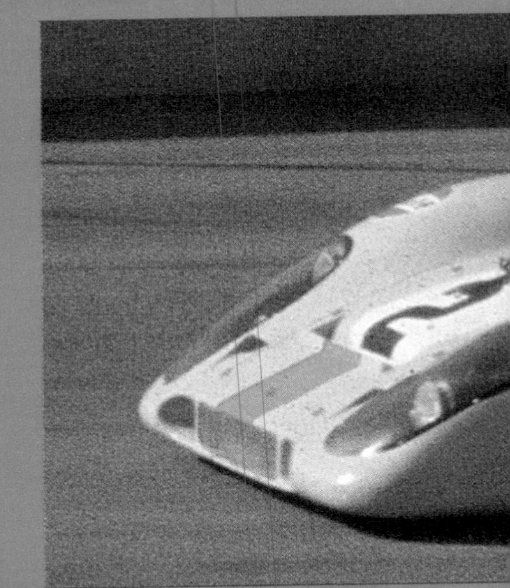

Gulf-Porsche
2
Gulf

Introduction

''In the case of a racing car, not only the driving but also the designing is fun''.

Thus concluded Dipl.-Ing. Hans Mezger's paper 'The Development of the Porsche Type 917', presented to the Institution of Mechanical Engineers in January 1972. Certainly, over the period 1965—'72 Mezger had enjoyed an ideal climate in which to design racing cars as the head of Porsche's newly-created Konstruktion Rennfahrzeuge. The racing car design group was a division of Dipl.-Ing. Ferdinand Piëch's Experimental Department. In his late Twenties, newly appointed Technical Director Piëch gave racing new importance in the priorities of the Zuffenhausen, Stuttgart-based marque.

Both Piëch and Mezger were young, creative and ambitious and Piëch, son of Louise Piëch, née Porsche (co-founder of the marque with brother

Ferdinand) had, or could find, the resources needed to turn dreams into reality. A gush of increasingly venturesome racing cars — painted traditional German racing white rather than Porsche's established silver — poured through the gates of the Zuffenhausen factory. For years little silver cars bearing the Black Horse of Stuttgart had contested the small capacity classes of major sports car races but Piëch wanted to win outright and, above all, dreamt of winning Le Mans.

The Porsche prototype leapt from 2.0 litres to 5.0 litres within three years, growing like a tropical plant within the hothouse environment created by the youthful, '65-founded Piëch regime. But one man's dream can be another man's nightmare. In '67 motor racing's rulers had decreed that prototypes should henceforth be limited to 3.0 litres — the capacity Porsche had just reached — in the interest of curbing speeds, particularly at Le Mans. However, they had left a loophole — by building 25 examples at the outset, a prototype constructor could employ a 5.0 litre engine. And that is precisely what Piëch did, employing some shrewd political manoeuvring to secure the necessary resources. The result, with its big air cooled engine, difficult early track behaviour and subsequent overwhelming success became a motor racing legend.

Proper exploration of that legend wouldn't have been possible within these pages without the guidance of its begetter. At the time of the book's research Doctor Ferdinand Piëch was Audi's Vice Chairman and board member for Research and Development — clearly a very busy executive. Nevertheless, he spared precious time to patiently answer questions on all aspects of the 917 story. Similarly, Porsche race car designer Hans Mezger and his colleagues, Racing Director Dipl.-Ing Peter Falk and Development Engineer Dipl.-Ing Helmut Flegl took the trouble to explain a host of details, shedding new light on a number of topics. Many others closely involved with the 917 programme also gave valuable assistance, as indicated by the list of acknowledgements. The authors are extremely grateful to one and all.

It would have been impossible to ignore the pioneering research of Paul Frere and Karl Ludvigsen in their splendid books, 'The Racing Porsches' and 'Porsche — Excellence was Expected', respectively, and other useful references were the autobiographies of John Wyer ('A Certain Sound') and Mark Donohue ('The Unfair Advantage'), plus the records of the period provided by *Sport Auto, Motor Sport, Autosport* and *Motoring News.*

As with the companion book 'Ferrari 312 & 512 Sports Racing Cars — The Porsche Hunters', this work concentrates upon the cars rather than the drivers, the technical rather than the political as it explores the story of the 917 as a works racing car. It is a fascinating adventure and the authors (Ian Bamsey and CanAm contributor Bill Oursler) sincerely hope that this account of it does justice to the efforts of all those who made the story possible.

...af, in colour: *...y days for the ...17 at the Ring ...er photo) and ... Mans in '69. ...Photo's: Nigel Snowdon.*

Pack den
in den Tank !
VEEDOL
BOSCH
12

Air raid

"The target was to help keep the Beetle competitive in the marketplace by showing the limit of air cooled engines". Grandson of Beetle creator Professor Ferdinand Porsche, Ferdinand Piëch admits that he enjoyed a very close relationship with Volkswagen and that the giant car manufacturer provided essential support for the 917 project.

"...Porsche alone couldn't have spent such effort..."

The go-ahead for the 917 was given in the wake of a reduction of the Group 4 Homologated Sports Car production requirement from 50 to 25 units. That decision, confirmed in April '68 to take effect from the start of the following season, meant that Porsche would be able to homologate its Type 910 2.0 litre Group 6 Prototype as a 'Sports Car'. With a policy of fielding fresh chassis for each major event and selling its surplus to privateers, the marque had taken its 910 production total to 28 over less than two years.

In '66 the 910 had been developed as a more sophisticated derivative of the first endurance car from Piëch's team, the Carrera 6. The uncomplicated, 911 engined Carrera 6 had been conceived as a 50-off 2.0 litre Group 4 racer, well suited to the needs of private entrants. In late '67 the 910 had been superseded as works prototype by the 907 with revised aerodynamics, then in '68 had come the 908 with similar chassis but new 3.0 litre engine. Thanks to the instigation of a 3.0 litre Group 6 Prototype capacity limit for '68, the 908 was the first Porsche with a large enough capacity to challenge for the coveted Le Mans victory.

But while Prototypes had been cut to 3.0 litres, Homologated Sports Cars had only been trimmed to 5.0 litres. Existing large capacity Sports Cars were powered by American stock block engines. The first 5.0 litre coupe with a racing engine to be homologated would have a massive power advantage. And power counted at Le Mans.

Group 6 regulations were to be revised for '69 with the removal of the existing 650 kg. minimum weight limit (150 kg. less than that for Group 4) and the abolition of the requirements for a full sized windscreen and road equipment (lights, spare wheel and luggage space), which would continue to apply to Group 4. Porsche was well qualified to produce a competitive lightweight spyder but a slippery 800 kg. coupe with a bigger engine would be far more competitive at the race that counted above all, Le Mans.

Star of the 1969 [Gen]eva show was a [pro]duction car with [L]e Mans winning [pot]ential. Available only as a 25-off [lim]ited edition, the [Po]rsche 917 had a [cl]aimed top speed [o]f 236 m.p.h. — [b]ut had yet to be tested.

"We had seen that Group 4 cars could be so much more competitive. It only needed a larger amount of money and Porsche could race 24 such prototypes (I had to sell at least one)", Piëch recalls. Work started in July of '68, only three months after the 908's race debut.

The 908 8 cylinder boxer engine had been developed without outside backing. Porsche historians often attribute its lack of sophistication to a concern that it should form the basis of a future production engine. Piëch shrugs off the suggestion: "there was no external help, consequently its elements were very simple... It was known that the 908 engine would be too expensive for mass production".

It is true, however, that the 908 unit was based on 911 boxer architecture (it was derived via an experimental chain driven four cam 911 engine, the 916) and it was considered that certain elements of the 908 — its four cam head in particular — might be relevant to future road car development. The race car engineering team was part of Piëch's 'Experimental Department', after all, and deliberately so. But major compromises

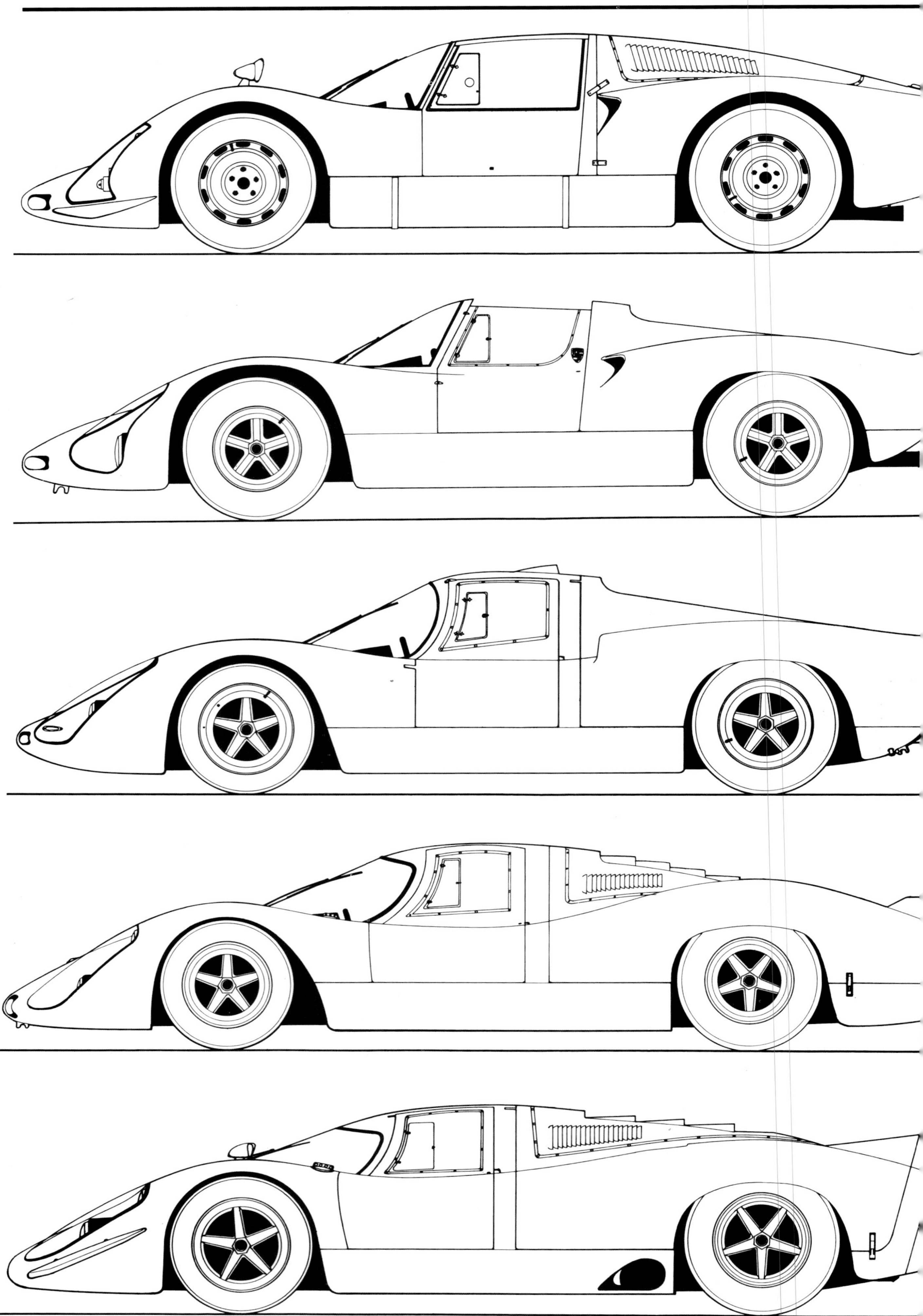

rdinand Piëch ht), creator of faster Porsche totypes, from rera 6 to 917. line drawings the evolution op to bottom) m the original era 6 through 10 and 907 of 7 (going from to 2.2 litres), e 908 of 1968 h 3.0 litres) to 7 (which, like 08 is shown in ional long tail Photo: Gulf. ings: Racecar gineering/*Bob Hine.*

of the 908 design — in particular boxer rather than more efficient 180 degree V12 configuration and vertical rather than horizontal cooling fan — reflected budget rather than policy considerations. The 908 was built to win, within the context of existing resources.

Thankfully the challenge of the largest capacity air cooled race engine ever could be tackled with a less restrictive budget. It was, however, necessary to retain a wide angle two-valve head at a time when others were starting to demonstrate the greater potential of the narrow angle four-valve head: the problem was the need for cooling air to be able to circulate around the valves. Consequently it was clear that a well designed water cooled four valve rival would produce higher power. "...And we were sure Ferrari would come in", Piëch reflects.

He explains that, with the target to keep the air cooled engine competitive, it was necessary to produce a light, aerodynamic car and to have a fuel consumption advantage. The 917 was designed to be light for better performance and better durability and to have good aerodynamics to help compensate for less power, both factors improving fuel consumption.

Better fuel consumption means fewer pit stops while lower drag means a higher top speed, and the possibility of overtaking on the straight. "It is much easier to pass on the straight", Piëch notes. Of course, light weight and low drag had always been central to Porsche racing philosophy. The marque had traditionally fielded small capacity cars and impressive advances in weight saving and drag reduction had helped compensate for a lack of muscle. Even the 908 had been conceived in such a spirit, rival manufacturers fielding significantly more powerful 3.0 litre engines. Understandably, the sciences of lightening and streamlining were taken very seriously at Zuffenhausen, in the suburbs of Stuttgart.

Exploitation of the boxer engine configuration was another Porsche creed. The earliest Porsche race car had been powered by a modified Beetle boxer and all subsequent Porsche race engines had remained faithful to the concept. With the 917 it was the hour for the time-honoured configuration to be abandoned. Piëch explains: "from our experience of the six and eight cylinder boxers we knew that internal ventilation was a major problem, not allowing us to reach the power of Formula One engines. The optimum solution was to put two con rods on one pin, creating a 180 degree V12".

With opposite pistons moving in the same direction rather than working against each other there was less inner compression: air pressure and turbulence in the crankcase were reduced, facilitating the creation of a good oil mist and reducing power loss. Further, with only six pins for the new 12 cylinder Porsche engine, the bearing requirement was reduced and it was possible to provide more robust webs and to increase the width of both big end and main

bearings (while still enjoying reduced frictional loss) to improve lubrication and reduce oil throughput. The only drawback was that of higher big end inertia loads, two reciprocating assemblies having to be stopped and started by a single pin.

Good balance was ensured by a crank configuration identical to that for an in line six, with each pin at 120 degrees from its neighbour, and pairing rods on each pin reduced the overall shaft length. However, due to the need for cooling air to circulate around each cylinder the bores had to be widely spaced and, with six cylinders on either side, shaft length was still such that calculations suggested that torsional vibration could be a serious problem. The only way to avoid the danger was to take power off the centre of the shaft.

The amplitude of torsional vibration of the shaft reduced towards the centre where there was a point of interference. Engine designer Hans Mezger positioned a power take-off pinion at this point, ensuring that the drive would be vibration free throughout the entire rev range. This was a major advantage for the camshaft drive, allowing a gear system to be employed without fear of a vibration problem. The central pinion was supported by a bearing either side, making a total of eight main bearings.

A significant advantage of the central pinion was that it left both ends of the shaft free to accept an axial big end lubrication feed. Previous Porsche engines had required an extra bearing to serve as a feed to the axial shaft drilling and as oil entered radially it had to have sufficient pressure to counteract the centrifugal force of the shaft. With an axial feed for each half crank pressure could be cut significantly, reducing the amount of power absorbed by the lubricating system. The system incorporated six scavenge pumps and was designed to be as dry as possible to minimise splashing losses.

The central power take-off necessitated a power output layshaft running under the rear half of the engine and accomodating this made the unit's centre of gravity higher. However, the layshaft could be designed to act as a torsion bar, compensating for heavy shocks in power transmission. There was also an upper layshaft driving various ancillaries, and the fan, which was put in the ideal position, above the engine.

A horizontal fan and an efficient oil system were both important measures given the challenge of cooling such a large capacity air cooled engine. Driven by gears, the fan absorbed 17 b.h.p. which compared favourably with the amount of power that would otherwise have been wasted pushing a water radiator through the air. Of course, having air cooling also saved the weight of water jackets and a water radiator system, but the 917 did carry a generous oil radiator.

Piëch agrees that the 917 was part oil cooled. "It is true that you have to get more heat out with oil than in a water cooled engine. But as in a water cooled engine the oil temperature is linked to that of the water, the oil is automatically much cooler".

Piëch notes that a water cooled block cannot be allowed to run at temperatures in excess of 120 degrees centigrade whereas on an air cooled engine the temperature of the fins can go as high as 160 degrees: "Porsche raced an engine with an aluminium crankcase up to 160 degrees centigrade..."

Having a magnesium crankcase, 128 degrees centigrade was reckoned to be the safe maximum for the Project 912 engine in long distance racing. The important point about the new engine is that its air cooling system was so efficient that it was actually *less* dependent upon oil for cooling than earlier Porsche engines.

The text book tells us that as the size of a cylinder increases the heat developed increases as the cube of the linear dimensions while the radiating surface increases only as the square, threatening a serious difficulty for the designer of the bigger capacity air cooled engine. Porsche had neatly avoided this by increasing the number of cylinders rather than cylinder dimensions. At the conceptual stage the possibility of using two horizontal fans, one for the front six cylinders, the other for the rear, was considered but a larger single central fan was a lighter, less complex solution that was just as effective.

Having a horizontal rather than the traditional vertical fan made it far easier to get equal air distribution to all cylinders. The early Sixties Porsche Formula One engine had similarly employed a horizontal fan, but had not been so well designed. Engine Project 912 drew on the experience of earlier engines and Mezger notes, "the efficiency of the engine was better so heat transfer was less for the same specific power output".

Whereas the superseded vertical fan engines had been around 30 — 35% oil cooled, with its more efficient horizontal fan Mezger estimates the 917 engine to have been only 15 — 20% oil cooled.

An interesting development for the new engine was the installation of oil jets to spray the underside of the piston. The piston cannot be

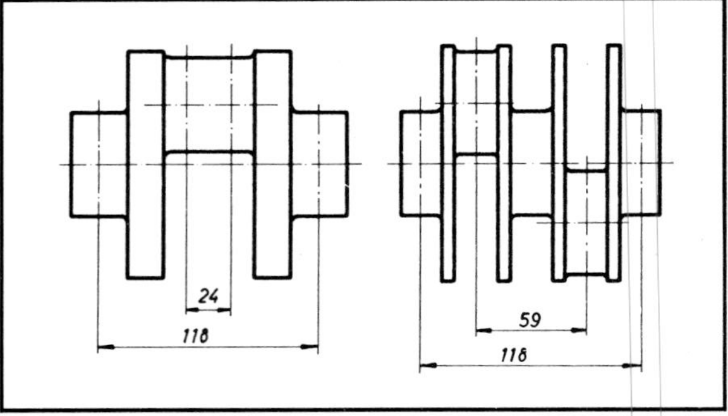

Comparative drawing showin detail of Porsc boxer crank wi one rod per pin and (left) equivalent port of new 180 deg V12 crank carr two rods per p (Porsche).

cooled by air and must consequently be cooled by fuel and oil circulation. As we have noted, the 917 was designed to be a particularly dry engine. It could be run without an oil spray to cool the piston but fitting 1 mm. diameter jets tapping 5 — 10% of total oil flow through the engine reduced piston temperature by 30 — 35 degrees. This allowed a 0.5 higher compression ratio to be run and reduced fuel consumption — Piëch estimates by 3 — 5% under race conditions.

If the 180 degree V12 configuration and the central power take-off were major innovations for Porsche, a third was gear drive rather than shaft or chain. "We knew gears would work from the outset", Piëch notes. He and Mezger couldn't afford to take any risks: 25 examples had to be produced straight off the drawing board. "At that time the engine was quite expensive, the whole car was expensive and the highest risk was the engine..."

Consequently, as far as practical, the 917 engine (code named Project 912) was derived from proven technology. Thus, the reciprocating gear, the cylinders (aluminium with chrome plated bores) and the two valve heads were adapted from the 908. Even 908 bore and stoke dimensions were retained, 85 x 66 mm. producing a total capacity of 4494.2 cc. The 917 would have such a vast power advantage that 5.0 litres could wait.

Interestingly, the bore size was the same as that

Porsche drawin illustrate ampli of fundamental and first harmo vibrations, emphasising be of central powe take-off.

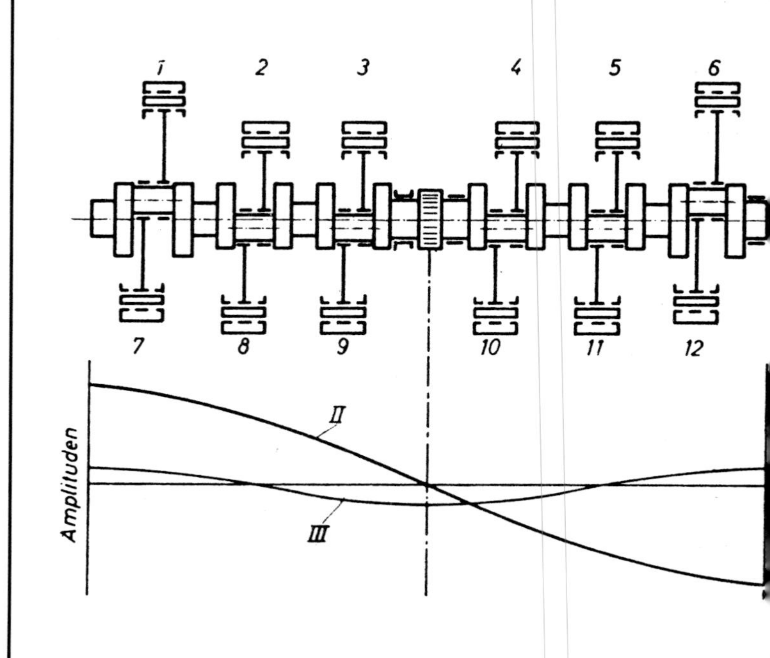

'impsed through rear window of he Geneva show ır — the largest ·acity air cooled ace engine ever.

of the contemporary 3.0 litre Cosworth V8 which was setting new standards in Grand Prix racing thanks partly to a well designed, gear driven four valve head. At 8000 r.p.m. the Cosworth engine had the same piston speed of 1,036 m.p.min. but a significantly higher mean gas speed: 101 m.p.min. versus 75 m.p.min. With narrow included valve angle, flat-topped piston and hemispherical combustion chamber, the single-plug Cosworth engine had excellent breathing and combustion characteristics and produced in the region of 150 b.h.p. per litre. With domed piston and chamber the contemporary twin-plug 908 engine was worth only 120 b.h.p. per litre. With Project 912 Piëch was looking for something better and one improvement was a slightly narrower valve angle for a more compact combustion chamber. But a well designed four valve head would always be superior.

As we have noted, one response was weight saving and this extended to the engine. Since the mid Sixties all Porsche race engine crankcases had been cast in magnesium. The alloy used was RZ5 which offered high heat resistance and good tensile strength. Although the linerless cylinders and heads were of aluminium, magnesium was reckoned to account for 29.5% of the total weight of the engine: magnesium (and the even more exotic titanium) were used as widely as possible. Titanium alloy Ti A1 6V4 was used extensively by Porsche, having the strength of first grade steel but only 57% of its weight. Even a titanium inlet valve was under development in co-operation with German piston specialist Mahle, the task being to develop a suitable surface treatment to overcome titanium's poor friction characteristics.

Co-operation with Mahle and Bosch played an important role in Porsche engine development and for Project 912 Bosch developed a new fuel injection pump, beating agreed delivery dates by an impressive margin, Piëch recalls. In contrast, the electrical side of the company was sceptical about the whole project and wanted only to supply off-the-shelf equipment. Frustrated, Piëch turned Instead to Marelli in Italy. The acquisition of a suitable 12 cylinder Marelli system spurred Bosch into somewhat belated action!

The 917 engine was conceived as a collection of sub-assemblies to speed development and subsequent race preparation. A mere five months after design commenced, in December 1968 all modules were ready and bench testing could commence. It took little coaxing for the power output to match the 908's 120 b.h.p. per litre with 542 b.h.p. The central power output's freedom from vibration and the careful design of the lubrication system paid dividends at this early stage.

Which was just as well, for less than 3 months after bench testing began the biggest air cooled race engine ever had to be dropped into its chassis. With the engine weighing 240 kg. it was no mean feat to get the car close to 800 kg., a lot of lightweight material having to be employed in the chassis. The use of titanium, for example, extended to the springs, roll bars and wheel hubs. Even the retention of the traditional 2300 mm. Porsche prototype wheelbase — which left the pedals ahead of the front wheel axis due to the length of the block — reflected the concern. Chassis engineer Helmut Flegl explains: "the main reason for the short wheelbase was weight. Make the wheelbase longer and you lose rigidity. To regain that rigidity means more weight. And with 800 kg. the target we didn't want any excess".

The chassis was derived from that of the 908 and like all Porsche prototypes since the Carrera 6 featured a multi-tube spaceframe, with lightweight g.r.p. body panels attached to it. Originally Porsche's frames had been fabricated from steel tubing but always it had been company policy to try to replace steel by a lighter alternative. It had taken a year's research, but with the 908 Porsche had been able to introduce difficult-to-weld aluminium tubing — both lighter and more rigid than steel. It required arc welding in an inert atmosphere which was provided by a shield of argon gas. All Porsche frame designs were subjected to a 1000 km. pave test as a matter of policy and were consequently durable, if not particularly rigid by the standards of a contemporary aluminium sheet monocoque. Nevertheless, that lack of rigidity wasn't considered a problem, and certainly wasn't seen as a serious drawback in respect of handling, according to Flegl.

Suspension was a straightforward outboard

wishbone-and-spring/damper system, carrying relatively narrow rims. Like the 908, the 917 was equipped with 15″ rims, only 9″ wide at the front, 12″ at the rear, whereas contemporary Formula One cars, which also ran on 15″ rims, carried 12″ fronts and 16″ rears. Porsche had always enjoyed the best chance of success for its nimble, low powered cars at the Nurburgring and the Targa Florio, unconventional mountain circuits calling for soft suspension with long wheel travel (twice that required at Le Mans where large spring movements are hardly in the interests of good high speed stability). With the wide, flat treaded tyres developed for Formula One in the mid Sixties a large amount of camber change would reduce contact surface and produce local overheating. Due to a lack of power wide tyres had not been imperative for Porsche, and running narrower rims reduced frontal area for less drag.

Designed specifically for low drag, the 917's shape evolved from that of the 908 coupe via extensive wind tunnel tests of 1/5th scale clay models and full sized mock ups at the Stuttgart Institute of Technology. Devoid of spoilers, with a clever optional, bolt-on Le Mans long tail extension it had a drag co-efficient of 0.33, 8% lower than that of the 908. It was a little lower than the 908 but a little wider and had a frontal area just 1.8% greater. It was calculated that it would reach 236 m.p.h. on Le Mans' three and a half mile long Mulsanne straight.

Low drag and high speed intensify the challenge of stability, lower drag making a car more sensitive to lateral aerodynamic forces. Side forces can be countered by careful location of the centre of pressure and the addition of stabilising fins but the influence of lift forces is harder to check. The slippery Sixties coupe was acutely sensitive to pitch: an inevitably slight amount of negative lift at the front could easily be converted into a significant amount of positive lift by a relatively small pitch change. More negative lift would be found at the rear, where any change to positive lift would make the car undriveable.

More worrying, at speeds approaching or exceeding those of light aircraft, was the danger of sufficient positive lift at the front to make the car take off. A number of flying incidents had occurred in the Sixties, at circuits as diverse as the Nurburgring and Le Mans. To counter the threat Porsche developed stabilizing flaps, based on the principle of aircraft trim tabs. "Porsche didn't want that sort of flight", Piëch recalls, "the flaps were an easy solution to keep the car down with no extra drag on the straight".

The trim tabs extended from the tail of the car, one either side of the deck. Front flaps were evaluated for the 917 at the design stage — they were found of marginal benefit and were perceived as vulnerable to damage in race conditions. The rear flaps ran flat under stable conditions but were linked to the respective upright via a bell crank system so as to respond to changes in pitch, generating negative or positive lift proportional to the degree of suspension movement up or down. The flaps raised as the rear suspension was extended (as under braking) and lowered as it was compressed (as under acceleration). Lowering the flaps raised the tail to help counteract nose lift, the idea always to maintain constant pitch. In addition to the flaps, the 917 was designed with 50% anti-dive to further check pitch variations. In theory, under cornering the flaps should have helped counter roll aerodynamically but the effect of this had proven insignificant on the 908 coupe which had pioneered the system.

While the 917 was able to adopt the 908 system of flaps in response to the challenge of its high speed potential, it required a new braking system: none was available from supplier ATE to match the projected 236 m.p.h. potential. ATE consequently developed a suitable system with four pot calipers and thick, radially ventilated discs.

Another new feature of the 917 was its in-house transmission, no existing Porsche gearbox being strong enough to handle the torque. As all previous racing transmissions from Zuffenhausen, this featured synchromesh, at the cost of slightly slower gear changes. However, the synchromesh was Porsche's own system, which it sold under licence throughout the world. Using it in its racing cars made good marketing sense.

The first 917 rolling chassis, like the engine, was ready to run in March '69. At this stage the Experimental Department was still based at Zuffenhausen but a move to Weissach was anticipated. Out in the countryside, Weissach offered a skid pan, while two test circuits (a 1.6 mile fast circuit plus a 1.8 mile mountain course sharing a common loop) were under construction and were due to open later in the year. The Experimental Department under Piëch's control employed 800 of whom only a small proportion were fully concerned with racing. Helmuth Bott was Piëch's most senior racing engineer and Mezger's design and engine development team reported directly to him while Flegl's chassis development team reported to Peter Falk, who in turn reported to Bott.

The race team was managed by Rico Steinemann, a former driver and journalist. It regularly comprised four or five cars. The principal drivers were Swiss Grand Prix driver (for the Rob Walker Lotus team), Josef Siffert, British rally ace, Vic Elford (recently retired to concentrate upon racing), veteran works driver Hans Herrmann and fellow Germans, Gerhard Mitter and Rolf Stommelen. They were supported primarily by Britons Brian Redman and Richard Attwood and Germans Kurt Ahrens and Udo Schutz.

The size of the team reflected the impressive way in which all aspects of the Porsche endurance racing programme had been developing since the start of the Piëch era in the mid Sixties. However, it took more than numbers to ensure success and che developed raft-style trim to stabilize its drag race cars ie late Sixties, tab movement responding to suspension movement, as cated by these che drawings. 'abs were seen e Porsche 908 e prior to the ich of the 917 op photo) and fitted to both and short tail ns of the new 4.5 litre car.

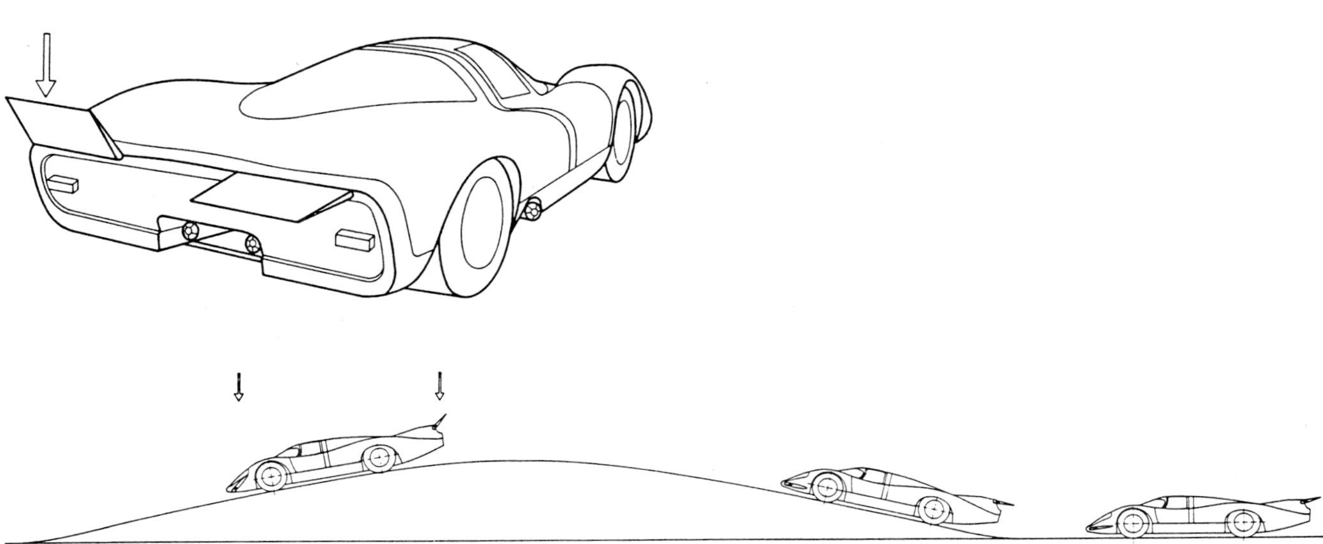

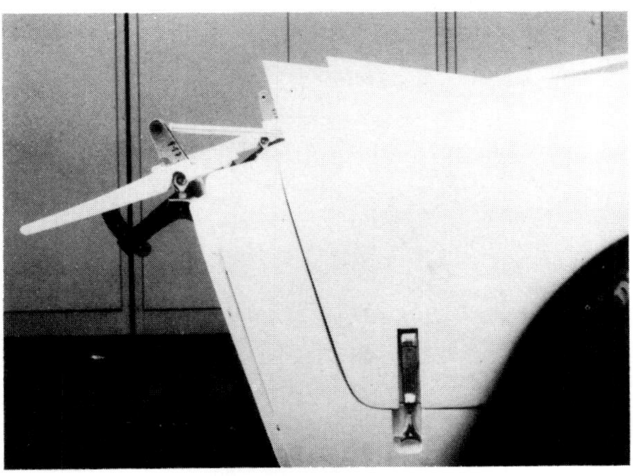

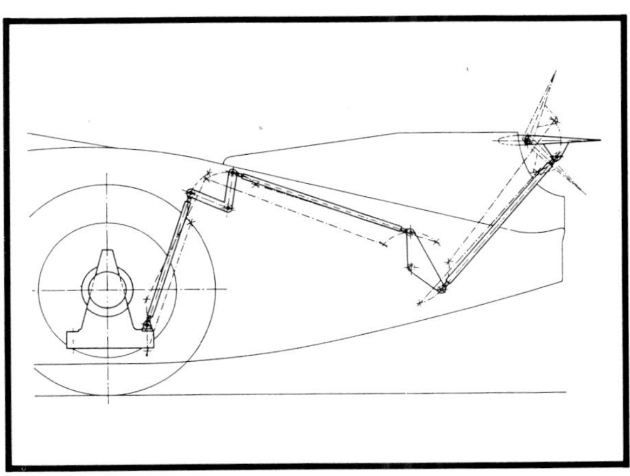

'68 had been a lean year. The new regulations had swept away the battles between 7.0 litre Fords and 4.0 litre Ferraris and had left 3.0 litre Porsches racing cumbersome 5.0 litre Fords. Porsche should have dominated the season and won Le Mans but too often had suffered an uncharacterisitic lack of reliability. And that trend continued through the first two races of the '69 season, at Daytona in early February and Sebring in March.

At Sebring Steinemann made an initial approach to the J.W. Automotive (JWA) team which was running the outdated, overweight stock block Group 4 Fords so successfully. Piëch had decided to sub-contract the race programme: "in war the best engineers for developing weapons are not the best soldiers. JWA was the best team and Porsche had the best engineers..."

Piëch saw a liasion with JWA as a rational marriage. He rejects the suggestion that he was pressurized into the concept: "I got the money and I had to win. It was left open as to whether we made it through such a marriage or 100% internally..."

In any case, there would be no marriage until the end of the existing season. With two races run and two races lost there was a lot of work for the 908 equipped Zuffenhausen operation to make up. But there had been a shock for its rivals just one week before Sebring, at the Geneva Motor Show. The 917 had been kept a closely guarded secret: assembled for the first time in early March, the first example had been taken to the show and unveiled on Press Day, March 12. It had been shown with a DM 140,000 price tag (£14,000/$35,000) and a sales catalogue. There was talk of the 25 car run having cost a staggering DM 8,000,000.

When the CSI had allowed Group 4 a 5.0 litre maximum capacity limit it hadn't anticipated accommodating anything other than existing American stock block engines. Prototypes had been restricted to 3.0 litres to cut speeds, particularly at Le Mans. Yet it now found itself being asked to homologate a brand new 4.5 litre Porsche prototype, a car that promised to take Mulsanne speeds to new heights...

The inspection took place while the show car was sitting in the glare of publicity at Geneva. On March 20 CSI representatives arrived at Werk I, Zuffenhausen to find three complete cars, 18 in various stages of assembly and sufficient parts to bring the total to 25. Porsche wanted homologation from April 1 so as to be able to take the car to the Monza 1000 km. race. The CSI refused, insisting that 25 complete cars was a prerequisite of any Group 4 homologation. Immediately every spare technician and mechanic in Werk I was put onto the job of rush-assembling the remaining cars and the officials were asked to come back in a month's time. There could be no race debut before May but, while the rush was on for homologation, on March 29/30 was the Le Mans test weekend...

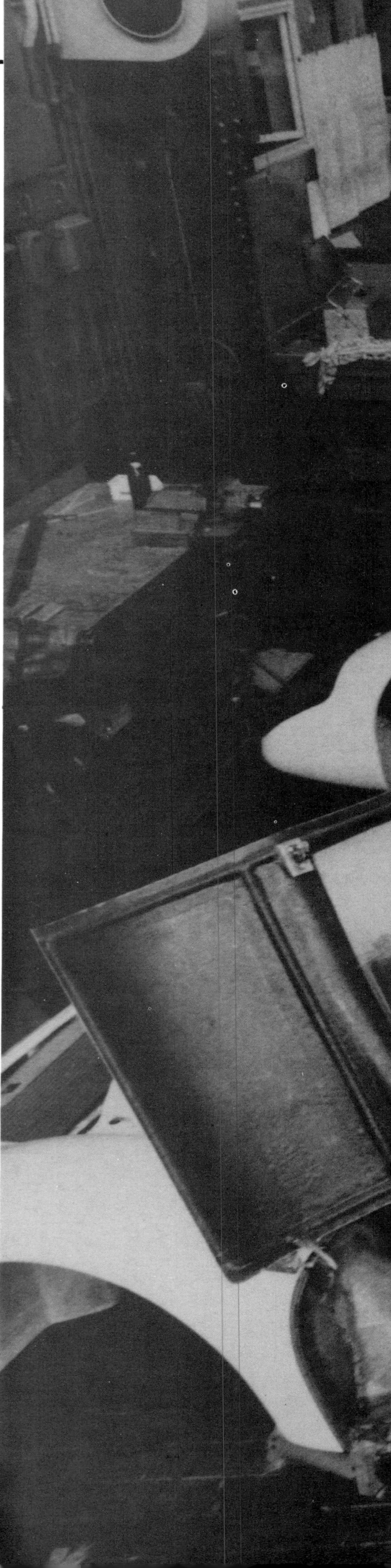

The C.S.I. refused to homologate the 917 on the basis of three cars plus parts from which the mandatory total of 25 could be completed — hence this production line set up in Werk 1, Zuffenhausen, in late March 1969 (Porsche).

Smooth, light and dry

180 degree V12
85.0 mm. x 66.0 mm. = 4494.2 cc.
Air cooled
Dry sump
Magnesium crankcase, aluminium cylinders and heads
8 main bearings, plain
Chrome plated cylinder bores
Steel crankshaft, 6 pins
Titanium con rods
Mahle aluminium pistons, 3 Goetze chromed aluminium rings
Double overhead camshafts, gear driven
2 valves per cylinder, 2 plugs
Bosch capacitor ignition
Bosch indirect fuel injection
10.5:1 compression ratio
542 b.h.p. at 8,400 r.p.m.

The novel crankshaft for engine Project 912 was forged from chrome-nickel-molybdenum-alloy steel (17Cr Ni Mo 6) and case-hardened to meet the requirements of the central power take-off pinion which was produced as an integral member. The entire assembly, with its six 48 mm. thick pins and eight 30 mm. thick main bearing journals, was 794 mm. long. Its pins were of 52 mm. diameter whereas previous Porsche shafts had employed beefier 57 mm. pins, the thicker webs allowing the reduction in the interests of reduced frictional loss. The forging was the work of a local company, Alfing GmbH.

The crankshaft ran in plain bearings supported by a vertically-split crankcase. The two bearings either side of the central pinion were of 66 mm. diameter while the others were of 57 mm. diameter. The case also carried the bearings for the power output layshaft which ran under the rear half of the crank plus those for a full length ancillary-drive layshaft which sat above. Space under the front half of the relatively high mounted crank was taken by the dry sump system's main oil pump (run from the lower layshaft's drive gear). The pump was mounted in one half of the case and oilways were cast and drilled in the other half, the sealing between oil gallery ports and communicating pump ports being effected by O-rings.

Both layshafts were driven directly off the central pinion so there were only three main gears in the case. The output shaft's drive gear had 31 teeth whereas the central pinion had 32 as gears last longer if the teeth in mesh are not always the same. It consequently ran 3% faster than the crank, losing 3% torque. The ancillary drive shaft needed to run at crank speed as it drove the distributors and altenator. The power take-off layshaft ran in a roller bearing either side of the 31 tooth gear and a ball bearing at the output to the clutch. It was a 22 mm.-diameter steel shaft and was designed to act as a torsion bar. The ancillary shaft ran in four ball bearings. Bearings for the engine were supplied by S.K.F. and Ina.

The case was sand-cast by Honsel GmbH in magnesium alloy RZ5 (American designation ZE 41A). It was held together by 16 bolts passing across its entire width, above and below each main bearing. Finding the right bolts to tie the case together, and to attach the aluminium cylinders to

ᴧn air cooling ·m, with large ᶅ fan, ducting widely spaced, ned cylinders, Porsche's 180 ᵵe V12 engine a bulky unit. 'heless, it was vely light and produced omfortably in excess of 500 h.p. from the set (Porsche).

the case, presented a design problem; steel and titanium bolts being unsuitable due to differences in thermal expansion. The solution was found in Dilavar, a special steel alloy with a co-efficient of thermal expansion similar to that of magnesium and aluminium. The separate bolts attaching the individual cylinders required an insulating sleeve so as to remain unaffected by the cooling air flow, and this was of g.r.p.

In addition to the through bolts, the nuts of which were provided with special stress-relieving spherical washers, the case was tied by short bolts passing through the lips of its two halves. Assembly of the crankcase consisted of laying the pump and three shafts, with attendant gears, in the righthand side of the case and then bolting on the other half: a relatively straightforward operation. Due to the pairing of rods, the offset between cylinder banks was smaller on this engine than previous Porsche engines, being half the 48 mm. width of the pin. The lefthand bank was offset ahead of the righthand bank. The spacing between bore centres was 118 mm.

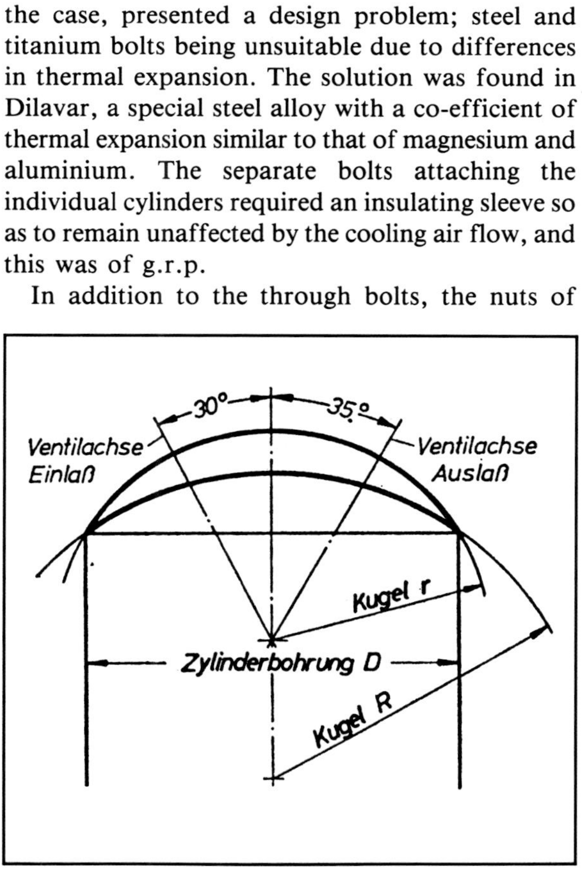

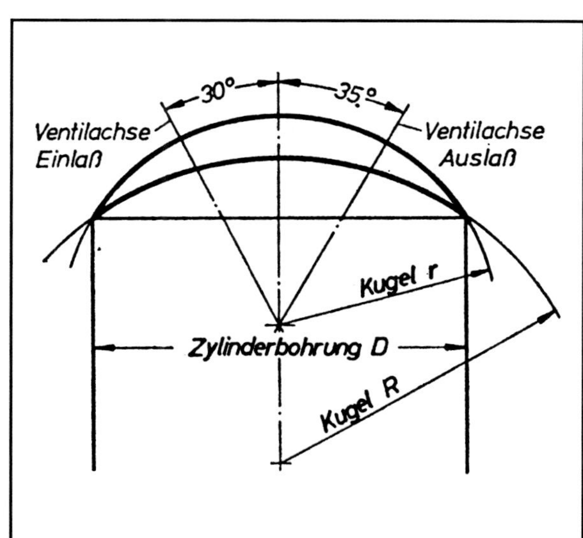

The 917 had convex piston and concave d forming an 'orange peel' combustion ber, as shown Einlass *means inlet,* auslass, *xhaust, while* achse *is valve axis,* lerbohrung *is der bore and means sphere (Porsche).*

The finned cylinders were forged from the same high-silicon aluminium alloy as the piston — Mahle 124 — and after machining the bore was coated with a chrome layer into which a multitude of pinpoint recesses were rolled. The recesses of the so called Chromal cylinder retained oil, improving running characteristics. The six cylinders that projected either side of the crankcase were grouped into two banks of three by a narrow gear tower. This carried the drive from the central crank pinion to the middle of each camshaft and tied the crankcase to the camboxes, which in turn linked the cylinders.

The crank was turned by robust H-section forged titanium (Ti Al 7 Mo 4) con rods, at 130 mm.

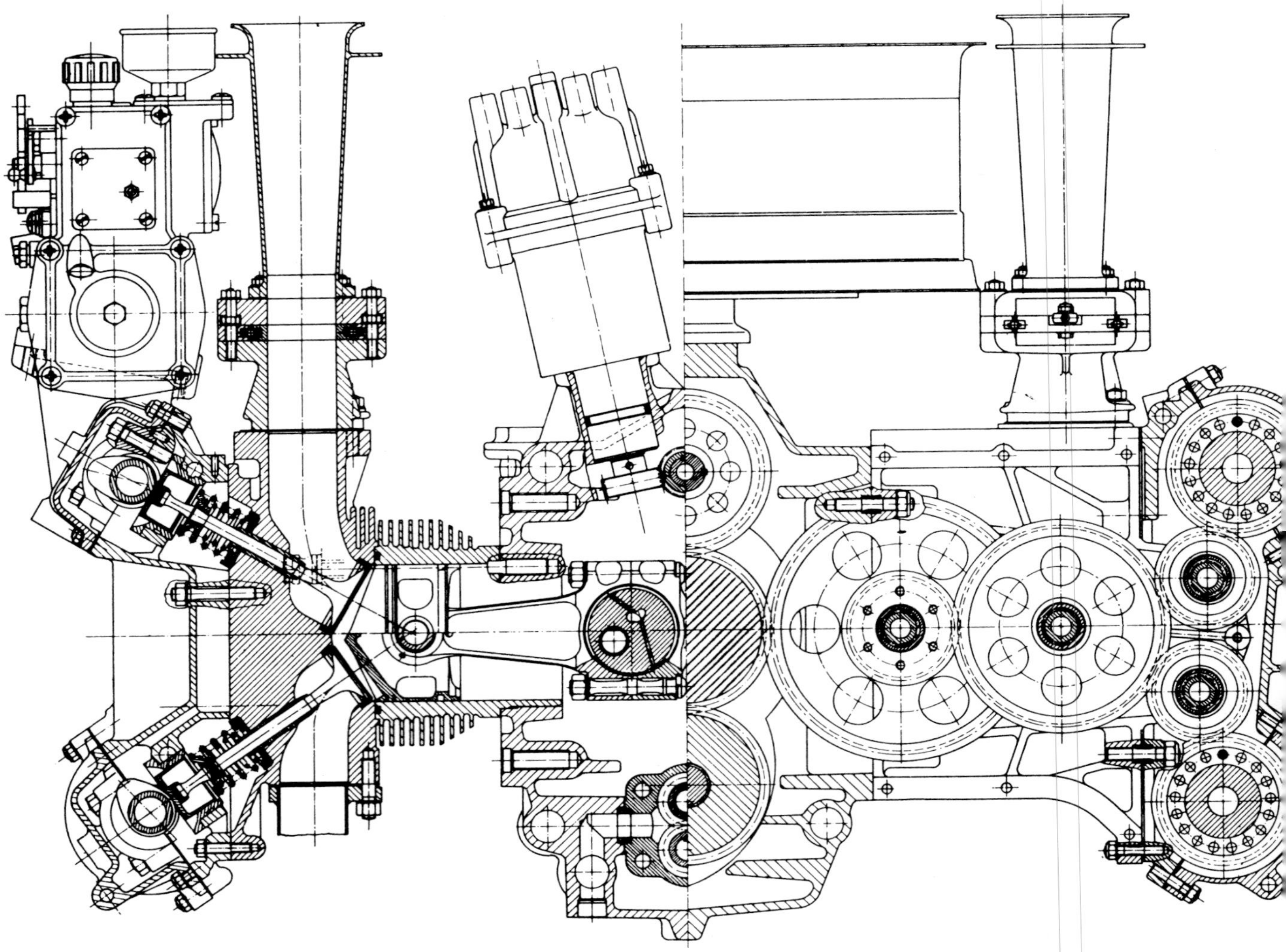

axis to axis the same length, and at 0.42 kg., the same weight as those of the 908, if smaller in big end diameter. Plain collar end bearings were employed to minimise oil throughput and the cap was secured by two titanium bolts with steel nuts. Any deformation of the bearing through stress or heat expansion was known to stress titanium less than steel, while at the same time it was known that titanium nuts on titanium bolts tended to undo themselves. The nuts were secured on the inner end of the big end to gain crankcase clearance.

The short skirted piston carried Goetze rings, two 1.2 mm. compression rings plus a 4.0 mm. oil ring which was set below the gudgeon pin. The piston head was spherical, with valve clearance notches. The combustion chamber roof was similarly spherical, forming an orange peel chamber. The two valves were at an included angle of 65 degrees with the projected axis of the valves intersecting in the centre of the projected combustion chamber sphere. The valve angle was narrower than that of the 908 engine (71 degrees) for a more compact chamber with better surface-to-volume ratio and was as narrow as possible given the need for cooling air to circulate.

The cylinder head was the only aluminium casting of the engine, all other castings being of the lighter magnesium. The individual heads were chill cast in an iron mould from a heat resistant alloy. The 41 mm. inlet port fed down into the combustion chamber from a horizontal manifold above the inlet valve, which was inclined 30 degrees above the horizontal cylinder axis, while the exhaust fed down from the chamber to exit below the exhaust valve which was set at 35 degrees. The head was attached by the four shrouded Dilavar cylinder capscrews and between head and cylinder was an O-ring gasket, allowing metal to metal contact to provide good heat transfer.

Cross-sections engine Project (Porsche).

Drawing to sho Dilavar cylinde and crankcase (Porsche).

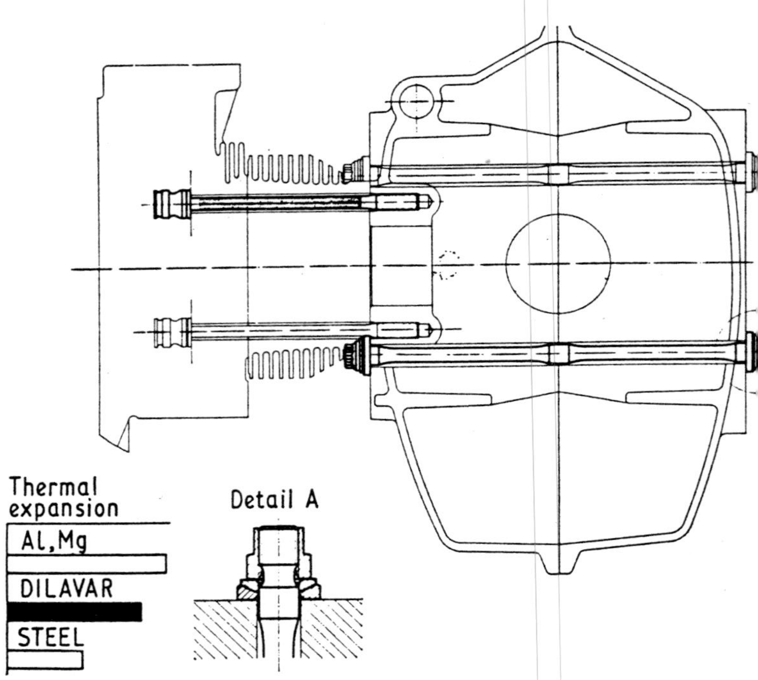

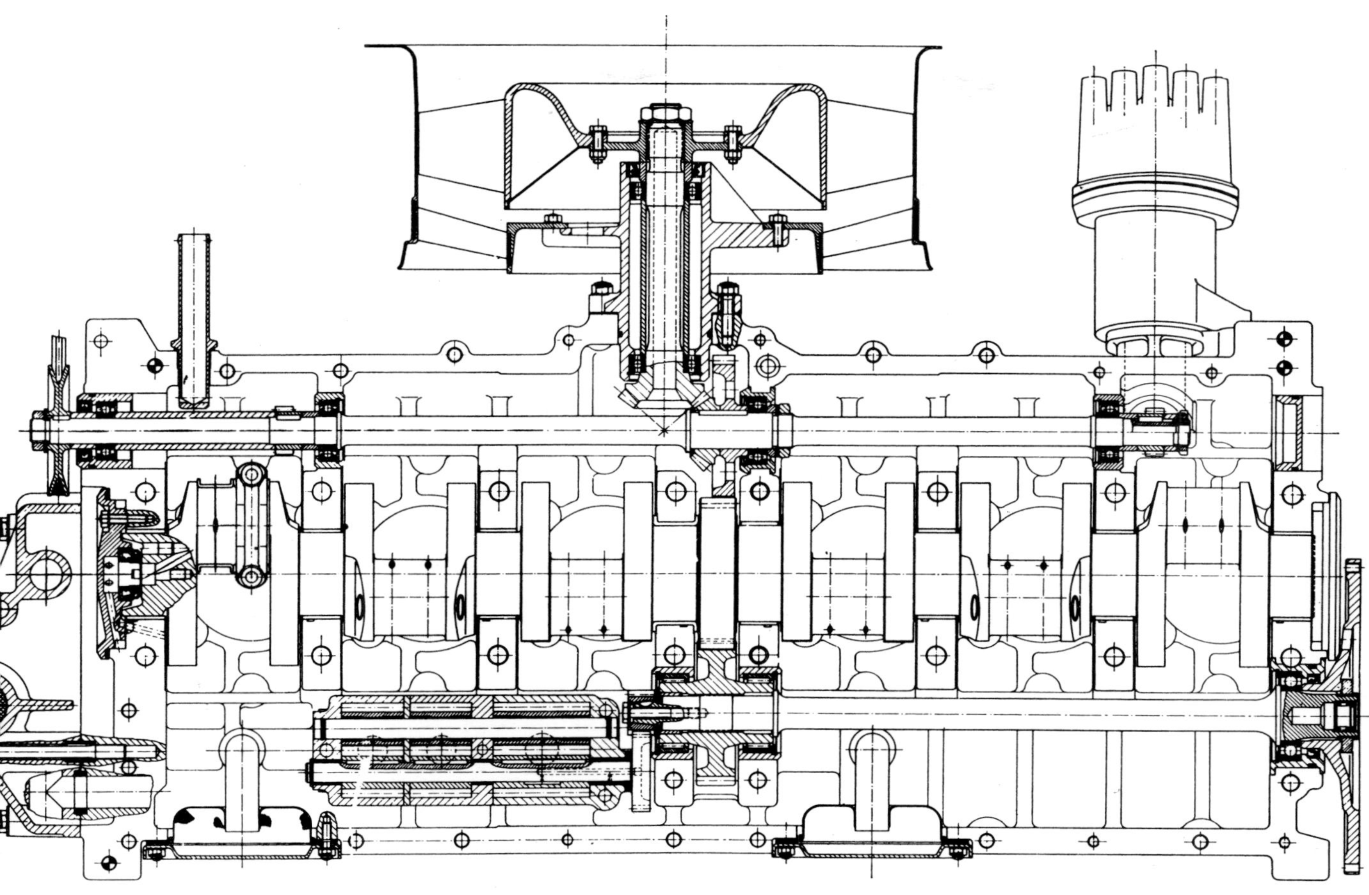

Longitudinal ion of engine Project 912 (Porsche).

The head was equipped with cast iron valve seat inserts and cast iron valve guides. The valves were of nimonic steel and were hollow and sodium filled to aid heat dissipation. There were two coil springs on each valve stem, made from vacuum-melted alloy steel wire. The inlet valve was of 47.5 mm. diameter with lift of 12.1 mm. The exhaust valve was of 40.5 mm. diameter with lift of 10.5 mm. Valve timing was 104/104/105/75. Maximum valve acceleration was calculated as 0.0134 mm./sq. degree cam angle, maximum deceleration as 0.0056 mm./sq. degree.

With only two valves per cylinder there was room for twin ignition, the platinium electrodes of the two plugs protruding into the chamber and positioned for short combustion paths. Porsche claimed the 912's chamber was notable for small surface, showing no fissures and inducing an optimum combustion process, as indicated by the late ignition timing of 27 degrees b.t.d.c.

As noted, the six individual heads on each side of the engine were connected by a common camshaft box. This was a magnesium casting, as were the cam covers that closed it, one for each hardened steel shaft. Each shaft ran in eight 30 mm. diameter plain bearings. Shaft drive was via five intermediate steel gears running on needle roller bearings carried by the aforementioned self-contained, narrow cast-magnesium gear tower. The camshaft drive gear was clamped against a collar on the camshaft by a large threaded nut. The relationship between gear and collar was established by a pin inserted through one of 17 bores in the gear and one of 16 bores in the collar. This differential permitted an exact and straightforward valve timing adjustment at the fully assembled stage.

The camshafts operated the valves through steel bucket tappets which reciprocated in light alloy bushes inserted in the magnesium cambox. The valves, springs, tappets and retainers were identical to those of the 908. The lefthand inlet camshaft drove the new 12-plunger injection pump via a wide toothed belt. The pump was designed and produced by Bosch and had a plunger for each cylinder arranged in two banks of six in a magnesium housing. The fuel quantity was controlled by a three-dimensional cam which in turn responded to the position of the throttle slides and engine revolutions. The pump supplied fuel at an injection pressure of 18 kp./sq. cm. through nylon injection hoses. From plunger to injection nozzle the 2 mm. bore (6 mm. outside diameter) hoses were of consistent length.

The injection nozzle was mounted as high as possible in a tall g.r.p. induction funnel, injecting downstream. The funnel was attached to the manifold, which carried throttle slides. The slides were ball mounted to avoid sticking. Positioning the injection nozzle high kept the process of atomization cool for a homogeneous mixture, and to avoid the danger of accumulation of fuel above the throttle slides on over-run, the three-

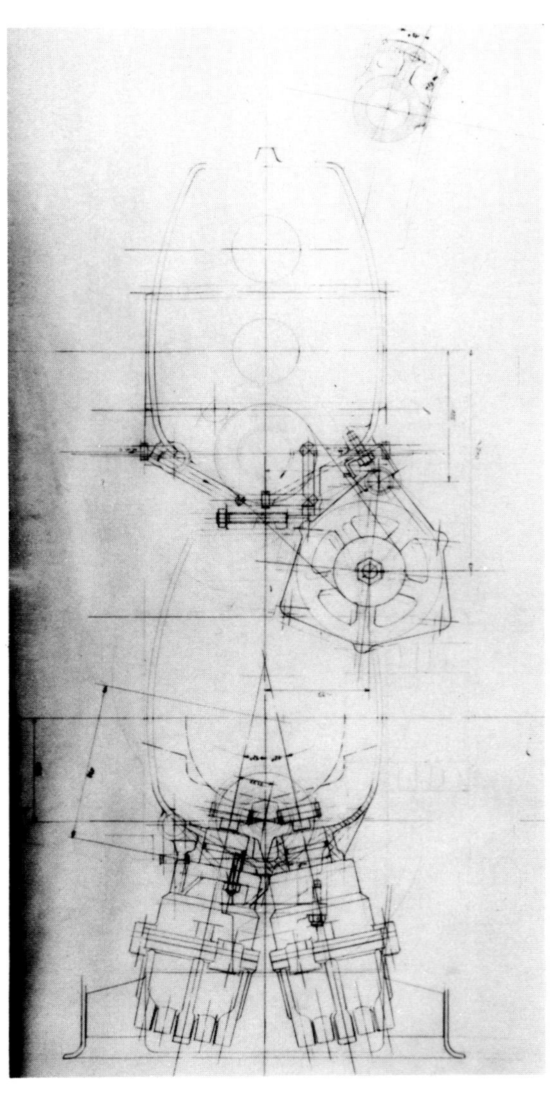

dimensional cam (which continued to inject the quantity required for idle even with the throttle shut) interrupted the fuel supply at engine speeds in excess of 4000 r.p.m.

Bosch supplied the entire ignition system, including alternator, two distributors and plugs (X 290 P 21). The 860 watt alternator was mounted opposite the fuel pump on the right of the engine, but inside the row of trumpets whereas the slim double-row pump lay outside. It was belt driven from the front of the upper layshaft and charged a 12-volt 45 Ah battery. The two distributors, sitting atop and one at either end of the crankcase, were likewise driven by the upper layshaft, but in this case directly by skew gears. Each distributor was set into a different side of the case, sloping 12 degrees from vertical towards its side, and fed its respective bank. The ignition was a capacitor system and dual-circuit, so there were four ignition circuits.

The firing order was 1 - 9 - 5 - 12 - 3 - 8 - 6 - 10 - 2 - 7 - 4 - 11: with equal firing intervals in each group of three cylinders the exhaust system was simplified. Each group of three fed into its own megaphone. The megaphones for the front cylinders fed out at the sides, ahead of the rear wheels, while the same length megaphones for the rear cylinders fed through the rear of the tail.

The dry sump lubrication system featured seven pumps and a large, 30 litre oil tank in recognition of its role in cooling the engine. Three of the pumps, one pressure and two scavenge, were combined in the aforementioned main sump pump. Drive was via a 13/25 reduction gear screwed into the front end of the power output layshaft. The two 42 mm.-wide scavenge gear-type pumps serviced, respectively, front and rear portions of the crankcase. Both scavenge pick-ups incorporated a filter which was accessible via its own detachable circular cover in the crankcase floor. The 64 mm.-wide gear-type pressure pump fed through an assembly at the front of the engine containing an oil filter and an adjustable relief valve, which, returning oil direct to the pump, was set to maintain a constant pressure of 5 kp./sq. cm. for the crankshaft assembly.

Camshaft lubricant was reduced to a pressure of 3 kp./sq. cm. via throttle valving. A controlled oil feed to the tappets provided a 60% reduction in cam box throughput. A drilling feeding into each tappet guide was uncovered only when the cam pushed the tappet down: only at a valve lift of approx. 2 mm. was oil able to enter the bore. Four 11 mm. wide scavenge pumps — one at either end of each exhaust camshaft — kept the cam boxes as dry as possible, these pumps driven by the respective shaft.

The half dozen scavenge pumps returned oil to the large 30 litre oil tank. Oil was taken to it via a cooler whenever the oil temperature exceeded 85 degrees centigrade, otherwise a thermostat allow it to bypass the seven row radiator mounted in the nose of the car. There was a total of 45 litres in the oil system.

A 330 mm. diameter g.r.p. fan with six 58 mm. blades running at 0.895 engine speed supplied cooling air: 2400 litres per second at 8400 r.p.m. engine speed. Of that output, which absorbed 17 b.h.p., 65% cooled the heads, 35% the cylinders. The air ducts were formed from g.r.p. The fan was driven by bevel gears directly from the upper layshaft. It was secured to its drive by two 6 mm. titanium bolts. Titanium bolts, nuts and washers were used throughout this extraordinary engine, which weighed only 240 kg. in spite of its large dimensions. The unit measured 800 mm. wide (slightly narrower than the 908 thanks to its gear drive), 900 mm. long and 560 mm. high. and was reckoned to represent 160 hours of work to build up from component parts.

Project 912 ran a 10.5:1 compression ratio and was officially rated at 520 b.h.p., although power was already closer to 550 b.h.p. at 8,400 r.p.m. The engine was designed with a 1000 r.p.m. safety margin and Mezger is able to reflect that "from the start it was better in its mechanical behaviour than any previous Porsche engine. The central drive was the answer". With its vibration free power take off, rigid gear drive and inflexible valve actuation via bucket tappets, Mezger reckoned that the valve gear was "an optimum solution". He also noted that from the very start it had been very dry thanks to its improved lubrication system. With 25 examples already committed, Piëch and Mezger could breath a well-earned sigh of relief...

Left: Early ske… exploring layou… 917 ancillary drives.

Right: Internal… the extraordina… 917 engine exp… (Autocar/ Quadrant).

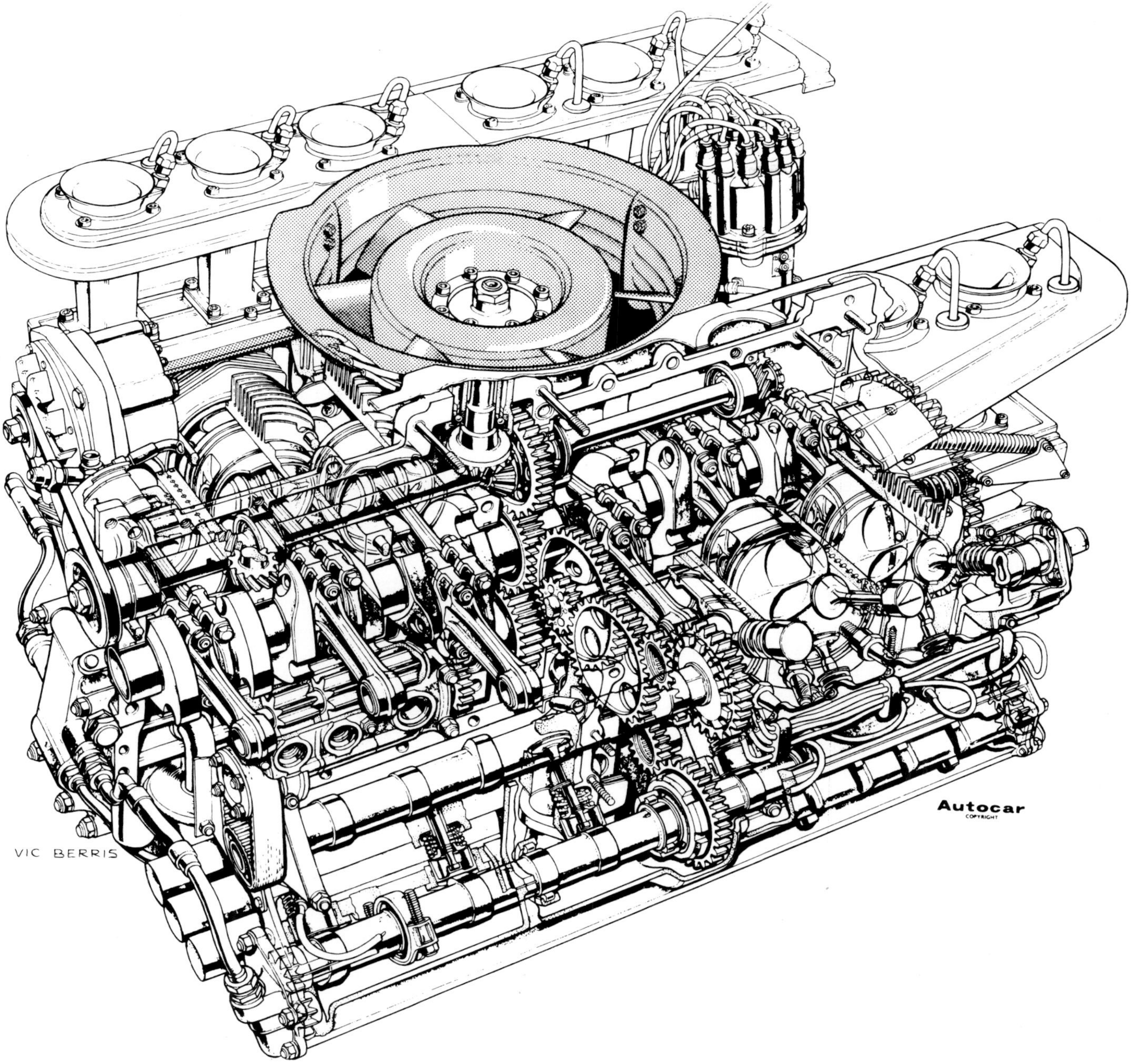

Autocar
COPYRIGHT

VIC BERRIS

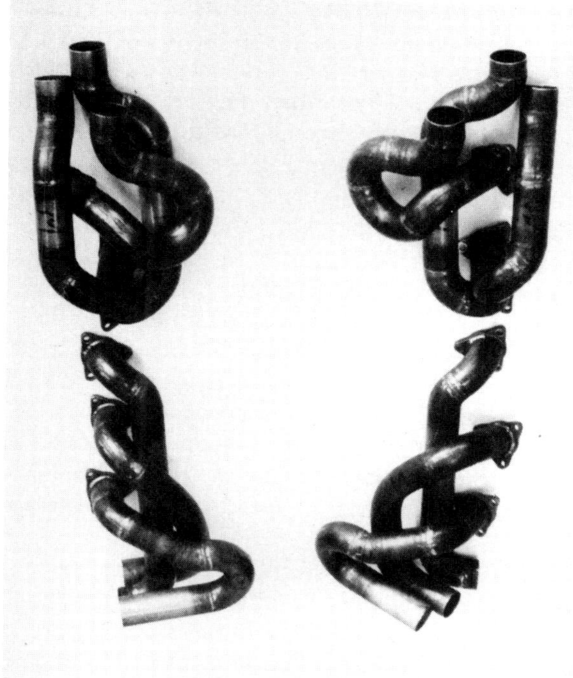

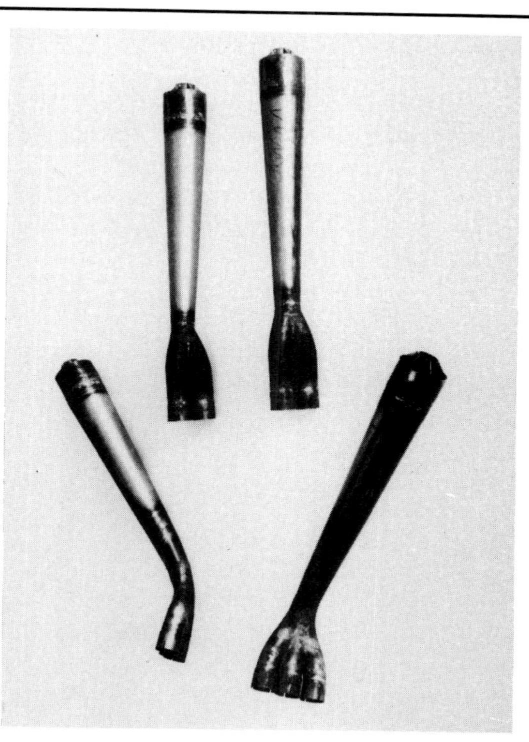

nplex exhaust m for the 917 Porsche). The ipes from the ront cylinders re routed out gh the side of the car, as ated overleaf.

Light heavyweight

Porsche aluminium spaceframe
Unstressed engine
Traditional suspension, Bilstein dampers
Porsche 15″ magnesium/titanium rims, 9″ front, 12″ rear
ATE 3050 mm. cast iron discs, outboard
ATE single, four pot calipers
G.r.p. bodywork
1 Behr oil radiator
Fichtel & Sachs 7¼″ triple plate clutch
Porsche 5 speed gearbox, ZF l.s.d.
140 litre fuel tank, 30 litre oil tank
Letta battery, Cibie lighting equipment
2300 mm. wheelbase, 1488 mm. front track, 1457 mm. rear
Dry weight 800 kg.

Porsche's new heavy duty transmission was a straightforward combination of triple plate clutch, outboard mounted five-speed-plus-reverse gearbox and ZF self-locking differential. The assembly was carried in a three-part magnesium transaxle casing cast in alloy RZ 5. Bolted to the crankcase, the bellhousing and differential case was in a single unit with the gear case and endplate attached to it. Prominent ribs added strength.

The clutch was a Fichtel and Sachs item with its three discs of only 180 mm. diameter due to the lack of clearance between the low output layshaft and the ground. The discs carried bonded organic linings. The starter ring gear was mounted on the clutch flywheel. A 0.9 b.h.p. starter motor was tucked in the transmission casing under the differential.

The feed from the clutch went under the differential to the lower of two gearbox shafts, each running in two roller bearings with additional ball thrust bearings with the front rollers. All five forward gears had Porsche split ring synchronization. Fifth gear was optional and was mounted behind the rear bearing to reduce the length of the shaft between bearings. Aside from the synchromesh the 'box was conventional in racing terms and was easy to work on. "It was a kid's job to assemble it", Cuoghi told the author.

Gearbox lubrication was simplified through the use of a wet sump in the interests of reliability. The consequently smaller, lighter pump helped compensate for higher churning losses. Oil was fed to the needle bearings that supported the free-running gears by the external gear-type pump (driven by the lower shaft) through hollow shaft centres. External oil lines (nylon) supplied the differential. An oil jet sprayed the c.w.p. There was no provision for a transmission oil cooler.

The differential was the ZF disc-type locker and was regularly run pre-loaded, with a 75% locking factor. Final drive ratios were 1:4.428/4.444/4.625/5.285/5.375: these were calculated as offering theoretical maximum speeds from 199 m.p.h. to a maximum of 236 m.p.h. for the slippery *Langheck*.

A pair of steel arms was carried by the bellhousing and these provided the rear support for the drivetrain. Its mounting was unusual in that, in addition there was only a single mount at the front of the engine. The frame was strong but

Porsche 917's ressive looks enhanced by menacing phone outlets either flank.

was low on torsional rigidity — perhaps as low as half that of a contemporary monocoque car with stressed engine. The figure quoted by Porsche is 50,000 sq. m. x kg., with around 10% of that contributed by the bonding of the body to the frame tubes. The g.r.p. body panels were not bonded on in a manner calculated to add greatly to rigidity.

The frame was a functional assembly with tubes stressed as far as possible in tension or compression. Cross-bracing was extensive. Tube dimensions varied according to load intensity. The material was aluminium alloy either 20 x 1.6 mm., 25 x 1.6 mm., 30 x 1.6 mm., 32 x 2.5 mm. or 35 x 3.0 mm. The larger tube diameters were used for the lower parts and the suspension support areas. The design was comprehensive, incorporating windscreen surround, roof supports and outriggers both ahead of the front wheels and behind the rear wheels to carry bodywork. A characteristic of all Porsche spaceframes was the pyramid-like framework at the rear, above the transaxle, which added useful rigidity. There was a similar pyramid- like structure at the front. After installation of the engine two tubes were added across the top of the engine bay for additional strength. The total weight of the frame was less than 50 kg. with all brackets attached.

Porsche used chassis tubes to circulate oil between the tank and the front mounted radiator. All the tubes were interconnected to allow for an air pressure crack detection test. Through a tyre valve the frame was inflated to a pressure of 2.0 bar and had to hold that for a given amount of time (gradual loss was inevitable through pin holes in the welds). Each frame was checked upon construction and thus rated, to provide a ready check in the field.

The firewall bulkhead was an aluminium sheet fitting and contained a window above engine height to provide rear visibility. Boxes to carry the fuel cells were also of aluminium sheet and sat either side of the cockpit, in the door sills. The bonded-on 1.2 mm. thick g.r.p. body panels

ake disc with ot caliper by ATE, as ologated for ansportwagen 17 (Porsche).

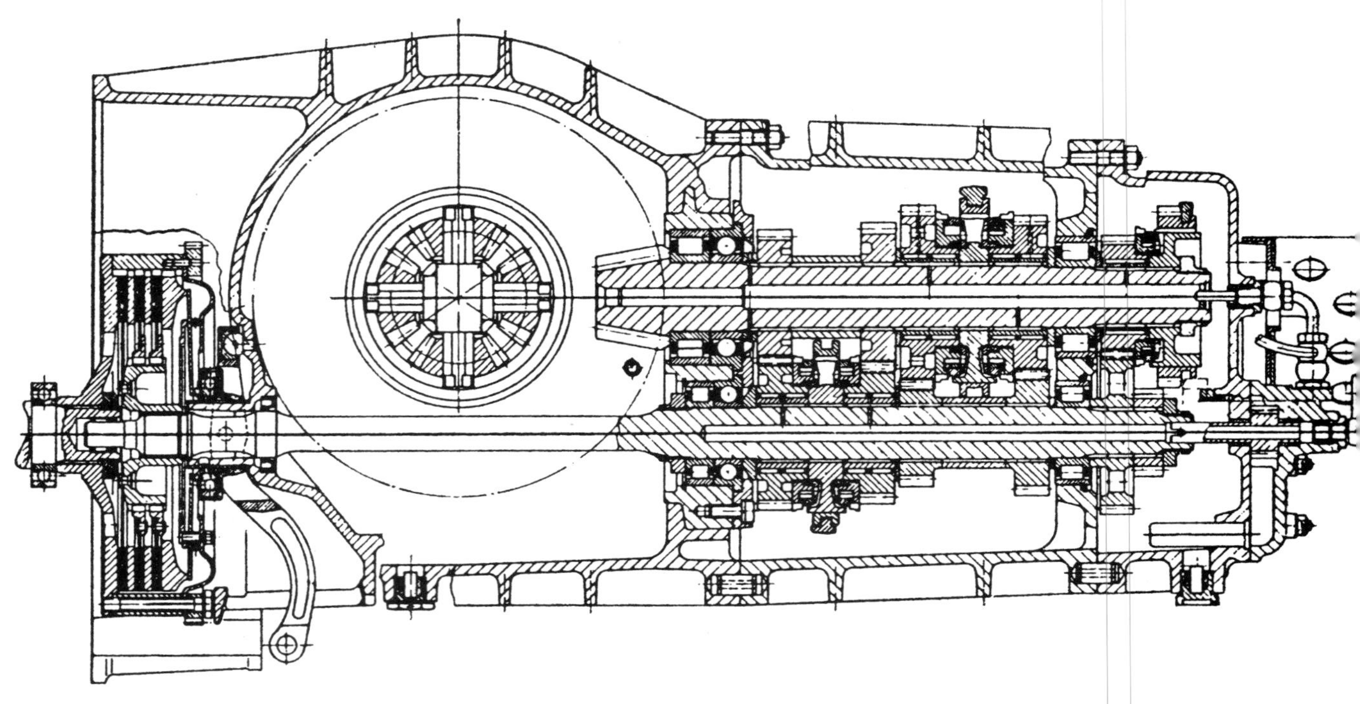

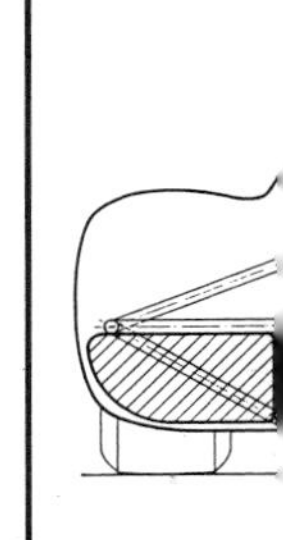

917 chassis technology: gearbox sectio (top), front suspension (le rear suspensio (below), fuel arrangement (and cockpit la (far right) (Po illustrations).

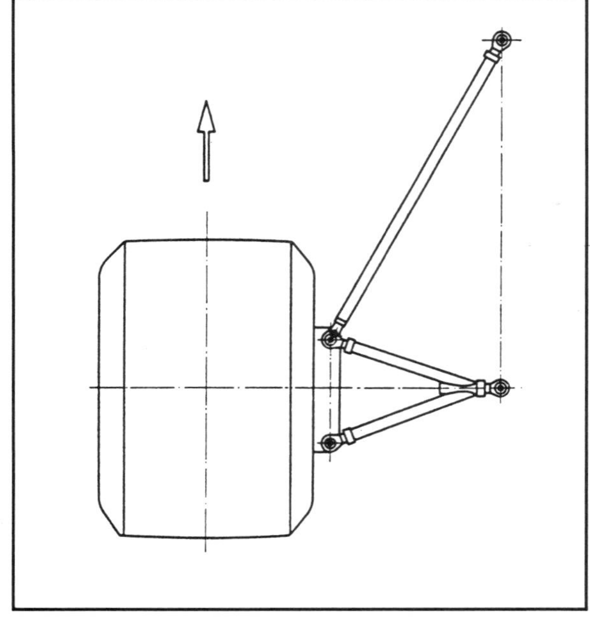

comprised nose-cum-cockpit surround (only a central nose panel was detachable, for access to the master cylinders and oil radiator), sills and undertray, rear arches and tail endpiece, the span of the tail being hinged. The hinged tail and door panels (hung at the front) were reinforced with aluminium tubes and contained Plexiglas windows. The windscreen was of 4.2 mm. thick laminated glass. The complete body, including g.r.p. seats and long tail attachment weighed less than 100 kg.

The front suspension was of conventional wishbone system with outboard spring/dampers. The lower wishbone was forward-braced to take braking forces in tension. The forward leg of the upper wishbone was, however, aligned with the wheel axis, as was the damper, which was slung between the frame and the apex of the lower wishbone. Front suspension geometry offered progressive rate and 50% anti-dive. Mounted upside down to save unsprung weight, the damper was a Bilstein light alloy gas-filled unit wrapped by a titanium coil spring.

The wishbones were produced from solid drawn aluminium piping while the ball joints had titanium housings. The uprights were cast in magnesium (with integral steering arms) as was the steering rack housing. The rack itself was produced from Aluknet, an aluminium alloy and offered a ratio of 11.4:1, so that there were only 1¾ turns from lock to lock. The turning circle was quoted as 13 m. Approximately 50% Akermann steering geometry was employed. The steering column was produced from titanium, as was the hollow anti-roll bar. The bar was mounted above the rack just ahead of the wheel axis and was swept back to link to the rear of the upright.

The stub axle was titanium with the wheel rotating on taper roller bearings and secured by a single central aluminium nut. The brake disc was driven by studs.

The rear suspension was of similar technology. The uprights were symmetrical and thus could be used either side and were carried by a reversed lower wishbone and a single upper link, with additional control by forward-reaching upper and lower radius arms. The wishbone pick up was under the transaxle while the upper transverse link picked up on the frame only a short reach from the upright. It was half the length of the reversed wishbone. The spring/damper pick up was nearby, the unit reaching down to the base of the upright and almost vertical. As a consequence of this progressive rate was produced by a conical grinding of the titanium wire rather than through suspension geometry. The tubular adjustable anti-roll bar picked up to the rear of the upright with arms swept back.

The driveshafts incorporated a cushioning Giubo rubber joint (or 'doughnut') and a ball race sliding joint and had a Hooke-type universal joint at either end. The sliding joint was mounted outboard of the Giubo joint which dampened the transmission during sudden torque changes. Together these two joints equalized changes in track length during upright movement. The two parts of the shaft which needed to be hardened on account of the ball races were forged in steel, while the rest was titanium.

The 917 was equipped with ATE cast iron discs

of 12″ diameter and 1.1″ thickness with radial ventilation channels. Each weighed 9 kg. ATE also supplied four pot calipers having two aluminium pots either side of a titanium bridge. The pistons were of steel, 34 mm. diameter and operated a total pad area of 600 sq. mm. The pads were 18 mm. thick and there was automatic adjustment for wear.There were separate master cylinders for front and rear brakes with a standard mechanism to adjust the front/rear balance.

The 15″ wheels were three-piece items produced by Porsche with magnesium rims and a titanium hub. The design provided five spokes and for five driving studs. The 9″ fronts carried Dunlop 4.75/11.30 — 15 tyres, the 12″ rears Dunlop 6.00/13.50 — 15s. A 15″ wide rear rim option was to be homologated. The car was set up with a small amount of negative camber front and rear and three degrees caster angle. Ground clearance was quoted as 100 mm.

Sitting between the wheels, the underslung fuel tanks were inter-connected by a large tube which ran across the cockpit floor ahead of the seats. Fuel fillers emerged to the rear of the front wings, feeding down into the forward end of the respective tank. Above the back of the righthand tank (behind the firewall bulkhead) was a collector tank. An electric pump brought the fuel up from each tank and a third supplied the injection pump. On the lefthand side was the 30 litre oil tank with its filler cap projecting through the tail. The Letta battery sat in the cockpit, behind the passenger seat, with the ignition boxes nearby on the firewall bulkhead. The coils were mounted over the transaxle.

The cockpit was starkly functional and adaptable. The driver's seat was adjustable for reach and the steering column was adjustable for reach and height. The seat was in two parts with the pan removable from the shell to allow it to be tailored to an individual driver. The steering wheel was of generous proportions and the seating position was only slightly offset to the right.

The instrument panel offered a central tachometer flanked by oil pressure and temperature gauges, visible through the steering wheel. To the left were warning lights to indicate low oil pressure, low fuel, high pad wear and lack of charge. There were also switches for the lights, wiper and fuel pumps, a control for the brake balance, plus an ignition key and ignition cut outs. The gear lever, linked by rods, was of titanium and moved through a new gate pattern for Porsche with 1st to 4th on an H pattern and 5th to the right and forward, alongside third.

There was a single windscreen wiper to sweep the large screen and twin headlights were provided, supplied by Cibie. The mandatory spare wheel, a Goodrich SpaceSaver, was carried on the rear spaceframe pyramid with mandatory luggage space carried by the tail either side of it.

The major cooling flows were the feed through the nose for the oil radiator and the intake through the rear window for the fan. The nose intake was notably small and the exit from the 600 mm. x 200 mm. Behr radiator was through a split ducting in the detachable front panel. The fan drew air in through slats in the gently raked rear window. Additional cooling flows were provided for the cockpit and the transmission via NACA ducts in the nose and tail.

The standard body, well streamlined with wedge nose, deep narrow windscreen rising between pronounced front wings, low (920 mm.) roofline (little higher than the front wings) and gently raked dorsum sloping down to sharply cut-off (Kamm) tail, was notably smooth and uncluttered by aerodynamic appendages, aside from the aircraft-style trim tabs extending from either side

of the tail. There was no rear spoiler, for example.

Extras to be homologated with the standard car included an alternative nose panel with larger (undivided) radiator air exit, front tabs and the 490 mm. tail extension, the weight of which was given as 12 kg. It was attached via four capscrews. Fins on the downward sloping extension held the trim tabs at the same height as on the standard car, the two flaps being linked by a (fixed) narrow aerofoil section. This was found to reduce drag, presumably by delaying air separation. Another option was a rear wheel arch extension to accomodate 15″ rims which added 60 mm. to the standard width of 1880 mm.

The quoted dry weight of the 917 was 800 kg, right on the class minimum and the weight distribution was approximately 40 — 60, front — rear. Approximately 5% of total weight was unsprung, while the engine accounted for around a third of the total. Even the modest homologated power rating of 520 b.h.p. gave it the impressive power to weight ratio of 0.65 b.h.p. per kilo — around 30% better than the contemporary class rival, the Chevrolet-Lola T70 (which weighed well over 900 kg.) and comparable to that of a contemporary Group 6 spyder. And in terms of sheer power, the 917 had at least a 100 b.h.p. advantage over all its rivals...

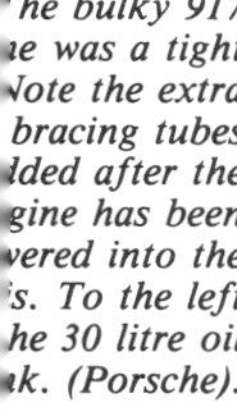

'he bulky 917 ie was a tight Note the extra bracing tubes dded after the gine has been vered into the 's. To the left he 30 litre oil ik. (Porsche).

Pot-pourri

When the 917 entered the fray the endurance race pace makers were Porsche's own 908 — run in either coupe or spyder trim, according to circuit — and the Ferrari 312P spyder. The Maranello challenger was significantly more powerful, utilizing the contemporary Ferrari V12 Grand Prix engine which offered approximately 420 b.h.p. as against 360 b.h.p. for the vertical fan cooled Porsche boxer. The Ferrari engine was a 60 degree alloy V12 with four valves per cylinder (at an included angle of 25 degrees) and chain drive. It had a seven-bearing, six-pin steel crank and steel con rods driven by domed pistons which ran plain rings in a plain cast iron liner. It was fed by Lucas fuel injection and was ignited by Marelli transistorized electrics. It was revved to 9,800 r.p.m., whereas the Formula One version was taken to 11,000 r.p.m. and gave a factory quoted 436 b.h.p. — which wasn't up to the strength of the rival Cosworth V8. That engine was to be employed in selected '69 endurance races by the JWA team, which had a new (Mirage) Group 6 chassis under development to replace its ageing Ford GT40s. The Ford was rugged but, while mustering no more power than the Cosworth, weighed over 1000 kg.

The Cosworth V8 had been designed as a sprint engine and was not yet proven in the endurance arena, whereas the Ferrari V12 was a derivative of

the marque's mid-Sixties, 4.0 litre Prototype unit. Another dual-purpose engine was the Matra V12, a four valve, seven bearing unit designed with Le Mans in mind. In '69 the Matra concern would concentrate all its resources upon the 24 hour race.

While the Mirage and Matra Group 6 cars utilised monocoque chassis, Ferrari employed a full tubular frame with alloy panels bonded and pop riveted to its centre section to provide rigidity approaching that of a monocoque. The V12 was heavily stressed in the back and, like Porsche, the marque had the advantage of being able to transmit power through its own transaxle. If the Ferrari had something in the region of a 60 b.h.p. advantage over the 908, equally it carried a hefty weight penalty compared to the spyder version: both cars came out with a power-to-weight ratio in the region of 0.61/0.62 b.h.p. per kilo. In contrast the power-to-weight ratio of the fastest rival Group 4 car, the Chevrolet-Lola T70, was less than 0.50 b.h.p. per kilo. The Lola's American V8 mustered something in the region of 430 b.h.p. but the car was on the wrong side of 900 kg. And dependable it was not.

The Chevrolet engine was a push rod stock block unit with a poor history of marathon running and the early record of the MkIIIB version of the T70 — new for '69 — was somewhat blemished by chassis failures. However, an example prepared immaculately by the ultra-professional Roger Penske Racing Team had been coaxed home to win the Daytona 24 hours after the big Porsche effort crumbled.

The Lola chassis was essentially sound, the T70 having a reputation as tough and good handling. It had been conceived by Eric Broadley after he had played a short but significant role in the genesis of the Ford GT40, still a factor in longer races, if less swift than the T70. The T70 had started life as a Can Am spyder with conventional front radiator, outboard suspension monocoque chassis. Its alloy tub had steel bulkheads and its side sponsons extended back behind the firewall to support the mandatory Chevrolet engine.

The Chevrolet-Lola had gone well as a Group 7 runner, winning the '66 Can Am series in Surtees' hands. The coupe version had arrived in '67 and had been homologated for Group 4 in '68 as a 50-off car, counting earlier spyders in that total. The coupe bodywork was in g.r.p. with fully detachable nose and tail. Its shape had been developed with reference to model tests in the Specialized Mouldings wind tunnel and compared to the rival GT40 was notable for a narrow cockpit superstructure (like the contemporary Porsches) and a high rear deck, mindful of downforce ahead of wind cheating.

e Lola T70 was a sound chassis that lacked a endable engine. Jevertheless, the Roger Penske cing Team took Chevrolet-Lola 70 to victory in opening round the 1969 World mpionship, the ona 24 Hours.

From white faces to victory

When the big red Porsche transporter disgorged two 917 coupés in front of a gaggle of impressed onlookers at the '69 Le Mans test weekend it was an anxious time for Piëch's team. The car had not yet run in anger. Indeed, the only 'name' driver to have sampled it was C.S.I. man Kurt Schild: he had taken it around the factory forecourt a week earlier, in the course of the homologation inspection. Since that first drive the only running had been a systems check, again within the Zuffenhausen gates. The first time for real was to be a very public affair.

Stommelen, Herrmann and Ahrens were on hand to drive chassis numbers 002 and 003, mostly in long tail trim. The test was a two day exercise during which the cars each ran around 400 kms. and suffered understandable teething troubles: a throttle linkage broke, there was a small engine oil leak, the wiper lifted at speed and, on the second day, a rear window broke up and was sucked into the fan with expensive results, but no injury to driver Stommelen.

Stommelen had fallen for the 917 at the Geneva show and wasn't one to be disconcerted by the general track behaviour of the car. The official factory report on the test doesn't make major comments on the handling but does record that the drivers were complaining of weaving on the Mulsanne. The problem was so severe that the car could not be run flat out, and reached no more than 199 m.p.h. It was, Falk told the author, "nearly undriveable". Nevertheless, pulling a maximum of 7,800 r.p.m. young Stommelen set a lap time of 3′30.7″, over three seconds faster than the best 3.0 litre prototype.

Chassis 003 was running in experimental trim with a sculptured, bulging sill shape and a slighly longer, flatter nose with smaller air inlets. On the second day it was tried with fins under the long tail extension, and also in short tail trim. In short tail form the report tells of even more severe weaving! Lesser problems to be tackled included a difficulty in starting the engine, insufficiently rigid brake calipers, overheating brake fluid and excessive heat in the cockpit. At this stage the model was reckoned to be very uncomfortable and some drivers were worried by the new gate pattern due to the potential consequences of an accidental shift from 4th into 3rd rather than 5th. That was a particular worry at the dauntingly fast Spa Francorchamps circuit, where the car next

mologation for 917 was finally ranted as from ay 1, following e inspection of is line up of 25 s at the factory late April. The el subsequently e its race debut n the Spa 1000 km. event — tured is Siffert n route to pole ition in chassis 005, which he eclined to race.

appeared, six weeks later.

Between Le Mans and Francorchamps 25 complete cars (finished with just one day to spare) had again been inspected at Zuffenhausen and homologation had been granted as from May 1. The hastily built examples were then carefully rebuilt...

Running from May 8 to 11, the Belgian 1000 km. meeting fell a week after the Targa Florio. It was bugged by persistent rain. Two 917s were entered, running short tail trim (in its early days the 908 coupe had proven more stable on sweeping bends in less slippery short tail trim), 003 (still with unique sculptured sill) and 005, to be used by Siffert/Redman and Elford/Ahrens as back ups to regular 908 coupes. Elford recalls, "both Siffert and I practised with the 917 and we both got out white faced..."

Due to the pressure of the big 908 programme there had been little time to attend to the 917 since Le Mans. Falk's subsequent press briefing on the meeting explained, "due to the constant rain during the three practice days we could not prepare the car properly. It was quite unstable and dangerous in the fast bends of Spa, above all with rain, and did not behave much better on the straight..."

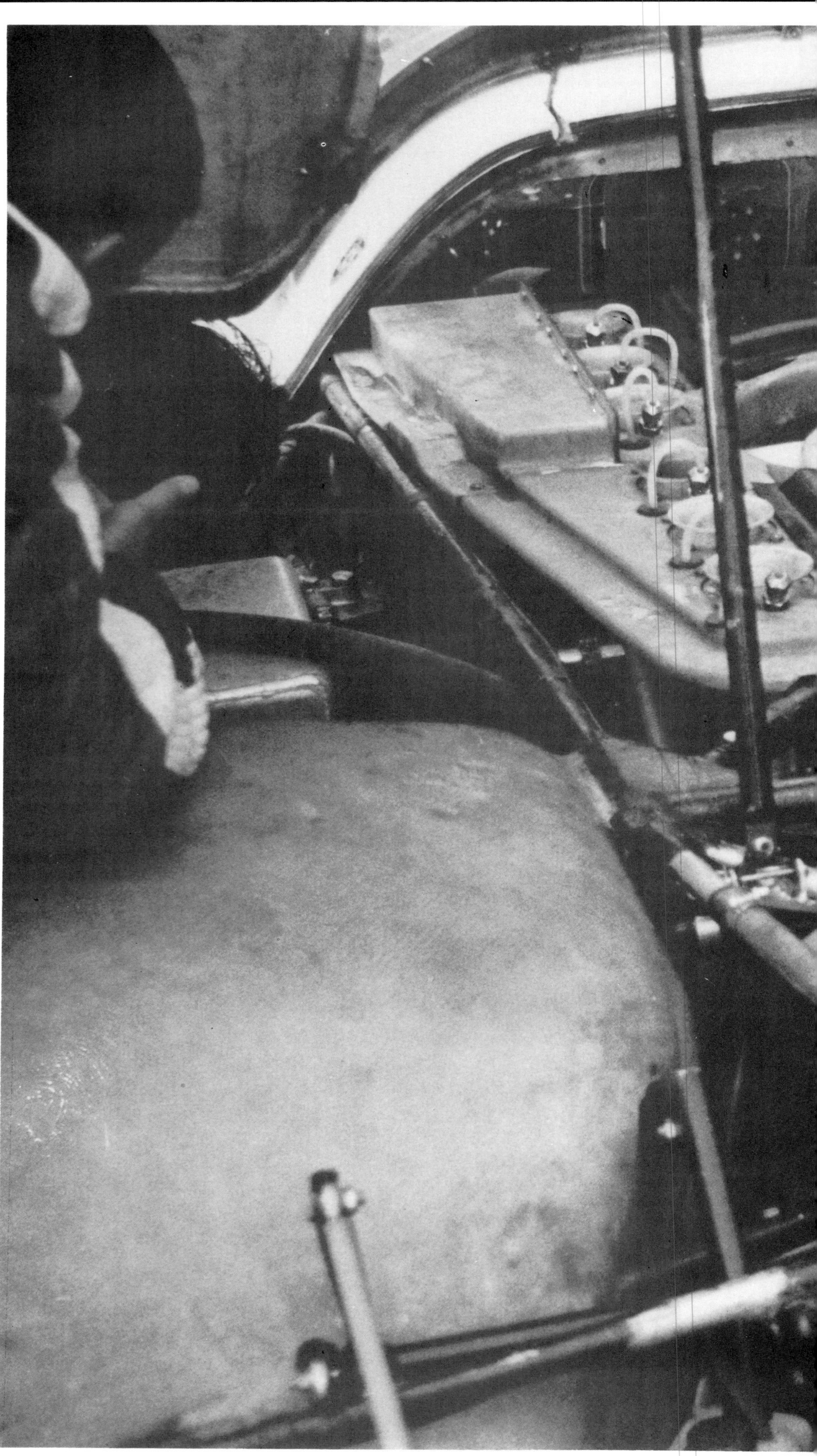

Centre of interest at Spa Francorchamps — a new Porsche prototype with a 50% larger engine! The spare wheel was mandatory for Group 4 and nestled on the rear pyramid.

The 917, as Elford recalls, required a lot of the width of the sweeping public road circuit. *Automobile Year's* man on the spot, Edward Eves, commented, "the car was proving almost unmanageable in the wet, not much better in the dry... Nevertheless, it was very fast, reaching 200 m.p.h. on the Masta straight. Siffert's fastest practice lap, which gained him pole position, at 3′41.9″ was as much a tribute to the driver's skill and bravery as it was to the car".

Siffert had taken pole from Hawkins' good handling Chevrolet-Lola by a mere 0.6 seconds and both he and Elford elected to race the 7 seconds per lap slower 908. However, Mitter agreed to race 005. Falk explains: "it was an adventure for him..." Sadly it was a short-lived one, the enthusiastic German ruining the clutch at the start and completing only one lap, the engine having been over-revved.

Between Francorchamps and the Nurburgring 1000 kms. on June 1 came the Monaco Grand Prix controversy over movable aerodynamic devices. The sole 917 taken to the event (004) had a short tail with trim tabs removed and a fixed full width rear spoiler added. It also ran sills without bulges, front tabs (a standard fitting for the rest of the season) and nose inlets ducting cooling air to the front brakes. This followed pre-race testing with chassis 003, which completed around 50 laps of the mountain circuit. Nevertheless, the model was clearly out of its element, particularly so early in its development. "We shouldn't have gone to the race", Flegl recalls, "the 917 still wasn't ready for a race and we had all sorts of problems".

The 917 again proved unstable at speed and was very difficult to drive on the winding course thanks to poor handling and braking. Falk's report said, "compared with the 908 spyders, the 917 behaved less flexible in the bends, more dangerous in the jumping zones and was not so easy to brake. Since every driver hoped to win the race outright, nobody was ready to drive the 917. Therefore we trusted Hahne and Quester with the 917 in practice".

On Friday Quester managed a best lap of 8′37.8″, some 37 seconds slower than Siffert's 908 pole time, although less than 8 seconds slower than Bonnier's best in the Group 4 pace setting T70. That evening the BMW board learnt that two of its young drivers were lapping in the difficult Porsche and put a stop to the exercise. Faced with a lack of drivers, Steinemann called in Piper and Gardner from England and they had to adjust to the car during a wet final practice session.

Steinemann's instruction for the race was to bring the car home at all costs. Driving for the first time in the dry, Piper completed the first lap in 13th place, down with the 2.0 litre runners, and at that careful pace the car was maintained. Running a long way adrift of the Group 4 winning GT40, it was lapped four times by the outright winner en route to a steady finish in eighth place.

Early days fo[r] 917 at Spa an[d] Nurburgring. [...] start at Spa s[...] the car get aw[ay] behind rival Chevrolet-Lol[a] (nos. 33 and 3[...] and the fastes[t] litre prototype[...] Cosworth-Mir[...] (no. 1), Ferra[ri] (no. 8) and tw[o] sister Porsche[s]. At Spa the ca[r] short tail spor[...] stabilizing flap[s] (below), at th[e] Nurburgring a fixed spoiler (right).

Chevron
CHAMPION
NSU
Chevron
MARTINI MARTINI
MARTINI
61
S
SHELL
PORSCHE

Lacking testing a natural agility, t 917 was a handf at the Nurburgri Note the holes t have been set in the nose to colle cooling air for t front brakes.

Mission accomplished — to Porsche's delight.

Just two weeks later came the big one: *Les Vingt Quatre Heures du Mans*. A number of developments were incorporated in the long tail cars run at the French circuit on this occasion, including modified suspension geometry to reduce anti-dive from 50% to 5% and a soft rubber mount in the steering linkage to put some slack between the steering wheel and the tie rods, the drivers having found it too easy to over-correct the car. There were also new brake master cylinders, wider air intake slots for front brake cooling and the car was run with more toe in.

Flegl says, "we found later by modifying the suspension that few of the early modifications were significant. But the toe-in helped a lot, and so did the steering rubber. However, the main improvement was that the car was set at a half a degree angle of attack. At the test weekend it ran flat and the nose lifted on the straight. So we dropped the front and raised the back, running stiffer springs, especially at the rear, to run slightly raked on the straight. We could now go flat out, although still the Mulsanne handling was not the best. However, it was OK after we fitted steep front tabs and changed the trim tab linkage so that the average angle of the flaps was higher".

Stommelen trimmed his best from 3′30.7″ to 3′22.9″. Aside from Elford's sister 917, only one other car could get within seven seconds of that time, Siffert's long tail 908 spyder. The newcomer had a tremendous performance advantage. But it had to be handled very carefully. Most disconcerting was the Mulsanne kink. Elford: "you couldn't go flat through the kink. And you couldn't just brake or you would unsettle the car too much. If you just took your foot off the throttle the car would be so aerodynamically unbalanced that the back would come up and take over.

"You know, the car steered a little bit like a boat. Once you lifted off at that speed the back end steered the car. The kink needed a gentle transition from accelerator to brake. Around 200 or 300 yards before the corner you had to ease off the throttle, settle the car — at over 150 m.p.h. the slightest lift of the throttle and you could feel the back of the car lifting — going gently onto the brake pedal before accelerating through the kink".

In contrast the full bore run from the two restaurants — where the car had just about reached its maximum velocity — to the approach to the kink some three kilometer posts distant was undramatic. "With your foot hard down, the car was reasonably stable. But the car did use a lot of road. We were 30 to 50 m.p.h. faster than the rest of the field but everyone was frightened by the 917 and kept well to the right..."

Rev counter readings suggested that the car was pulling its projected maximum speed of 236 m.p.h. but there is no official timing to support this. It was timed at fraction under 200 mp.h., at a point at which it was still gathering speed. Flegl reckons the genuine top speed was something in the region of 215 m.p.h.

A problem of tyre treads flying off was cured by increasing tyre pressures, while after practice the clutch plates were changed for an alternative type as the bonding of the linings was proving unreliable. Also the brake lines were re-routed due to a problem of fluid overheating. The factory report on the meeting also records that Stommelen wasn't happy with the brakes but Elford recalls no worries in that respect. "The problem of aerodynamic instability was the only worry. Once the car was poised in the braking mode it stopped pretty well".

The 917 was tuned to understeer and needed to be set up carefully for the corners: "You had to get it right first time, you couldn't change your mind. But if you set it up well it went through the Esses, for example, as well as anything else there".

Elford doesn't recall the stabilizers as particularly effective. Right from scrutineering they had been a source of major controversy due to the C.S.I.'s recent ban on movable aerodynamic devices. Porsche refused to remove them, given that they were part of the homologated specification, and the cars were allowed to practice with them while discussions took place between Steinemann and representatives of the C.S.I. and the organizers. Steinemann tried to secure the agreement of all the other entrants but not surprisingly the Ferrari, Matra and Bonnier Lola teams refused to go along with him. He threatened a withdrawal from the race, alleging that the car was dangerous without the flaps.

In an effort to convince the authorities Stommelen drove his car with fixed flaps on the second night of practice and showed that it was almost out of control. "He made a tremendous demonstration", Elford recalls, "and afterwards admitted to me that he had put on a show for the official observers..."

The important point is that Porsche had justifiable cause for concern over the car's high speed aerodynamic stability. In the end a compromise was reached. The 917 would run as homologated, the slower 908s with their similar flaps fixed.

Porsche had four 917s on hand at Le Mans this time: 006 as T car, 007 and 008 for Stommelen and Elford plus the first customer car for John Woolfe Racing. Apart from the chassis modifications, (which had been tested briefly by Linge at Hockenheim following the Nurburgring race) the cars had more powerful engines thanks to further development work. However, testing was still short for a 24 hour debut and Elford notes that Bott advised him against driving the unproven machine, reckoning it was unlikely to last the night. Elford, however, loved the car and felt a combination of its performance advantage and *very* careful driving could be a winning one. He consequently chose Attwood as a sensible co-driver.

Stommelen clearly didn't believe that the 917 could last. Right from the start he went out to put on a show. Alas, in his wake there was disaster on the very first lap.

Woolfe's car had been delivered direct from Stuttgart and co-driver Martland had only done two laps in practice before hitting the barrier at Terte Rouge. Overawed, he had decided to stand down so the factory had lent test driver Linge as co-pilot for the English amateur, who had a certain amount of experience of powerful sports cars but who did not have the credentials of a professional driver. It does appear that he had been a little too enthusiastic on the first lap, the most critical phase of the race with everyone keyed up and driving on cold tyres. In the company of top line drivers, Woolfe lost control under braking for White House. The car swerved into the barrier, overturned and slid along on its roof. As it broke with the violence of the impact its unfortunate driver was thrown out. Woolfe died on the way to hospital.

The race continued in spite of a large amount of wreckage on the track. It was a three-horse event in the early stages, only Siffert's 908 able to keep the 917s in sight. Driving with imprudent verve

ick Vic — he ed the 917 for its early vices, came close to Mans victory first time out.

af: the plant that e Mans mance back level of he xties 7.0 litre er cars hes in a clutch d, awaiting tion.

huiles
motul

14
BOSCH
CIBIE
SHELL
DUNLOP

Esso Esso
14

Stommelen went clear of Elford whose door had not been properly fastened. It stayed open an inch or so and he found he couldn't give it a good slam on the Mulsanne due to the aerodynamic forces. Hanging the tail out on sharp bends, Stommelen set a lap record of 3′30.6″ on lap six, while Elford stopped at the pits to have his door shut. Regaining second from Siffert, Elford set a new lap record of 3′27.2″, then resumed his softly, softly policy.

Soon after the hour mark the fuel stops commenced. Elford pitted after 64 minutes and was at rest for four minutes changing a wheel. Meanwhile Stommelen handed to Ahrens — who was back after one lap with an oil leak. The car was soon on its way again, Ahrens running reduced r.p.m. All of which left the long tail 908 (running almost ten minutes longer on its first (120 litre) tankful) to inherit the lead.

The order at 90 minutes saw Redman with a margin over Elford while the 908 coupes gave chase. The spyder was harder work than the 917, which had speed and acceleration over it. At this stage only Porsche was in it. The coupe bodied Ferrari (a conversion of the regular spyder) was disappointingly slow and the team had lost one of two cars in the wake of the Woolfe accident, and neither were the Matra Group 6 cars, the Bonnier Group 4 Chevrolet-Lola or the Ford GT40s in the picture.

Driven tenaciously, the spyder led for two hours. Then it retired, its all-enveloping rear bodywork having caused a high transmission temperature which in turn had melted external plastic oil pipes, seizing the gearbox. Elford/Attwood were left unchallenged. The sister car had lost around half an hour in the pits due to a broken exhaust. It was smoking and making routine oil stops. By the five hour mark it was eight laps behind.

As night drew in Elford was able to report that everything was perfect. By half distance, 2.00 am., the 917 had a comfortable four lap advantage over the 908s, the ranks of which had been briefly penetrated by a Matra. Meanwhile, the German crewed 917 had spent two hours in the pits having its clutch plates changed, reverting to the original type of linings. Insufficient spring tension had led to slip once the linings had worn to a certain degree and that in turn had casued the bonding of the linings to break free.

The sick 917 lasted until 3.50 am., then it had to be withdrawn, its linings broken free once more. However, the lead car sailed on serenely, extending its lead as dawn broke. The first sign of any trouble came at 7.00 am.: the car juddered as Attwood left the pits, suggesting a clutch malady...

At 10.00 am. the car was still running but sounding a little flat and trailing whisps of oil smoke. And the clutch was slipping. However, soon the last undelayed 908 broke and it was left with a ten lap margin over the second-placed GT40 of Ickx/Oliver, which now was catching up at the rate of around 10 seconds per lap.

At 10.45 am. the 917 was in for more rear end attention. Seven minutes were lost. And it was soon in again. Elford couldn't press the clutch.

Seconds after p.m. — Stom is powering hi into the lead Le Mans 24 h race while Sif takes the uniq 3.0 litre spyde alongside Elfo slower-starting Elford's door hadn't closed properly and soon require attention.

Previous p Stommelen's action at Le — note the angle of the tabs and th flaps in oper

Flegl: "the mechanics opened the rear cover and just put it down again..."

Flegl recalls that, while the team hadn't had great hopes for either 917 finishing, the race being treated as a development exercise, once the Elford/Attwood car had lasted the night it really did look as though it would go on until the finish. Elford felt that way, too. He and Attwood "had been driving slower and slower to conserve the car and by mid morning I began to think, 'we have done it, Mr Bott...'" Alas, the 917's new transmission let it down. The oil seal between the clutch and gearbox had failed and the bellhousing had cracked. "I felt we had been cheated..."

On the other hand, the performance of the 917 had been remarkable, given its lack of testing. There simply wasn't time for the newcomer in the midst of the big 908 programme. And that programme still wasn't plain sailing: having won the five European races prior to Le Mans, Porsche lost the big one to JWA by a whisker thanks to problems for all its cars. In July the 908s went to Watkins Glen to claim a sixth '69 World Championship win but the 917 didn't re-appear until the Osterreichring finale in August. And it hadn't been seriously tested since Le Mans due to the concentration on the 908, only running some laps on the Nurburgring south loop. This was another development exercise.

The 917s at the Osterreichring were entered in the names of clients who had taken up options to buy cars as the factory had officially announced its withdrawal, in anticipation of the marriage to the JWA team. Baron Karl von Wendt entered chassis 009, David Piper 010. Both were in short tail trim. The transmission casing had been polished to relieve stress raisers and the cast iron brake discs had been replaced by an iron ring disc on a steel bell to save weight.

Vents had appeared in the bodywork: louvres cut into the front wheel arches reduced pressure and improved brake cooling while a panel of aluminium louvres set into the tail sidepanels (alongside the engine) helped combat fuel vaporization. The car was run with front tabs and the single exit radiator duct, with a small lip ahead of the duct. It also had the rear arch extension, to accomodate 15 rear rims. The Osterreichring was a fast track but required plenty of grip for its long, sweeping corners. The rear flaps were set at a high angle and the rear roll bar was slackened off relative to the front.

The drivers didn't like the car, particularly the way it oversteered around the blind righthander at the top of the hill past the pits. Flegl: "we got it as best we could and Siffert tested it and said, 'its not handling as well as the 908 but at least its as fast...' I told him, 'Jo, you should race it, its time for a win'. He thought about it for some time. His preference would have been the 908 but he saw other reasons why he should drive the car".

Ahrens was paired with team leader Siffert due to his experience in the car while regular co-driver Redman shared the other car (010) with Attwood. To make life a little more tolerable for the 917 pilot, water cooled driving suits were now in use. Ice and water was tipped into a tank opposite the oil tank at each pit stop and this was piped through to the undersuit.

Two back-up 908 spyders were entered in the name of Porsche Salzburg, the Austrian Porsche distributorship which was owned by Piëch's mother, Louise. The principal opposition came from JWA's Cosworth-Mirage (a monocoque spyder based on contemporary Formula One technology) in the hands of Le Mans winners Ickx/Oliver, Bonnier's Chevrolet-Lola which he shared with Muller and a works Matra driven by Servoz-Gavin/Rodriguez. All three cars, in that order, qualified faster than the 917s.

Siffert rose to the occasion, battling Ickx for the lead in the early stages. It was sheer power versus handling and no-one else was in the picture as Ickx led to lap five, then Siffert led to lap 30, then Ickx took over again. The 1000 km. race would run to 170 laps. Siffert pitted for fuel on lap 38, Ickx on lap 41. The pursuing Lola and Matra ran to lap 43, at which rate they were on course to make it

...lford/Ahrens 917 pounds ...rough the Le Mans night, ...g the 24 hour ...with ease. But ...it has another ...ete revolution ...e clock ahead of it . . .

...af: scenes ...he ...eichring 1000 ...At the start ...o 917s were ... Bonnier's ...nd Ickx' ..., both of ...had Porsche- ...g potential. ... was that of ...n/Attwood ...e the louvres ...nt wing and ...nel.

through on three stops. The 908s had shown strongly in the early laps but had wilted quickly and the second 917 was already a lap down.

After the round of stops, Oliver led Rodriguez and Muller with Ahrens almost a lap down having had to do three laps with 140 litres on board while Ickx was lapping with low fuel. However, his times were a couple of seconds faster than Oliver was now managing in the replenished Mirage and he was soon past Muller (who wasn't driving as quickly as Bonnier had done following a major 'off' during practice). On lap 73 Ahrens regained second from Rodriguez, but was close to another fuel stop. Siffert went back in on lap 80 while Ickx took over the lead car on lap 86: three stops looked on for the Mirage, too. The frugal Matra and Lola went one more lap.

Although Siffert was able to slowly catch the Matra, which had slipped ahead yet again, Ickx was now lapping faster than the Swiss and looked sure to win. Bonnier had rejoined a lap down due to Muller's pace but was able to catch Siffert on the road.

On lap 99 it all ended for Ickx with a broken steering column bracket. Although being slowly caught, the Matra now leading had a fuel stop in hand over the 917. But five laps later it was on the side of the track, having spun into retirement following a missed gear change.

On lap 118 Siffert handed the leading 917 to Ahrens. The car required a left front tyre and proved reluctant to restart, needing neat petrol to coax it. Overheating of the fuel pumps had been bugging the cars throughout the meeting. Bonnier rumbled into the lead. On lap 130 he handed the Lola to Muller. The car rejoined 50 seconds down, a potential threat thanks to its superior handling and the fact that, unlike the 917, it could now run non-stop to the flag. The decisive factor was Muller's off-form performance. Ahrens was able to lap him before handing to Siffert, whereas he wouldn't have caught Bonnier. After a smooth stop Siffert had a comfortable run to the flag, finishing with over a minute in hand. Redman/Attwood came home third, a lap down.

Car 010 had a further airing in October, this time in the hands of Siffert and Piper, who had now bought it, at Fuji, contesting the unlimited capacity Japanese Grand Prix sports car race. The car ran in short tail Osterreichring trim under Steinemann's control and Siffert led the early stages but eventually big banger (Can Am) type cars from Nissan and Toyota came through to relegate the 917 to sixth. Since the Osterreichring Siffert had been racing a hastily modified spyder version of the 917 in the American Can Am series, always having to take a back seat to professionally run 7.0 litre cars. Nevertheless, the spyder version of the 917 did handle better than the coupe, as was emphasised soon after the Japanese Grand Prix at

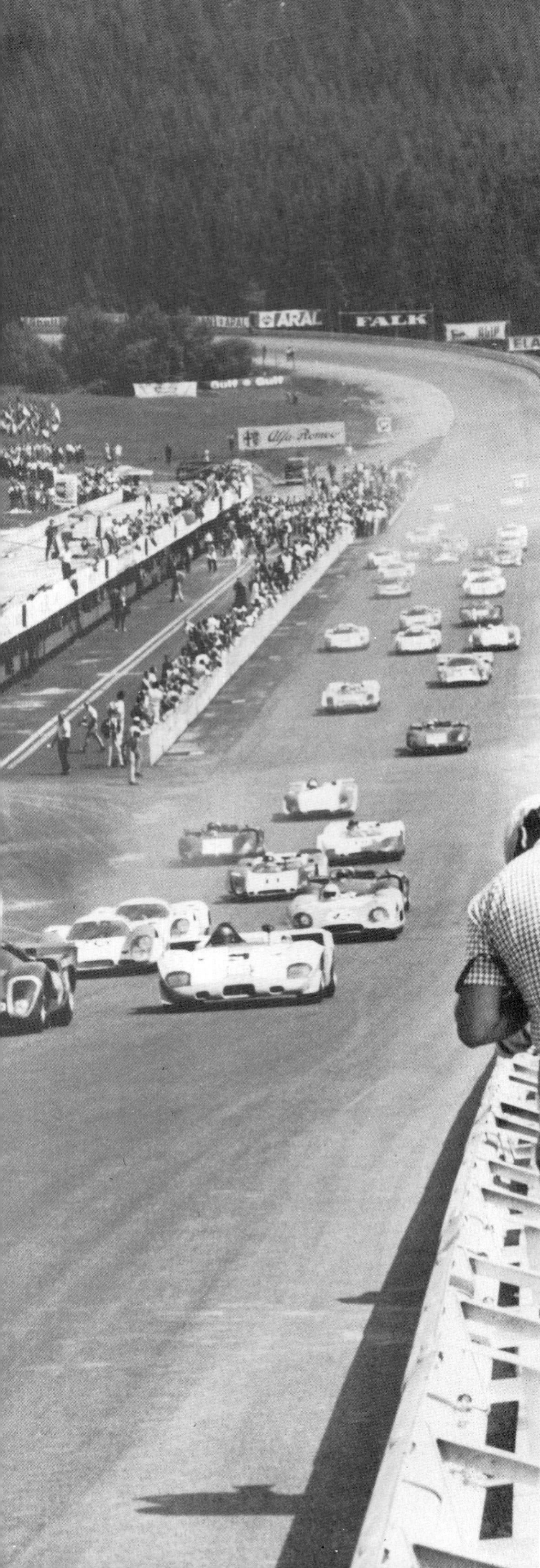

the Osterreichring where both a second, factory based spyder and a couple of coupes (006 and 008) were involved in tyre testing.

The Ostereichring test commenced on October 14. The 917 trio was driven by Ahrens and Redman and engineered by Falk and Flegl. The coupes were running in Osterreichring race winning trim, with stiffer springs to reduce pitch changes, and were still half a second adrift of the Cosworth-Mirage pole time, and were well behind the spyder which within a handful of laps managed to clock 1′46.4″ as against 1′48.2″ for 008, 1′49.9″ for 006. The spyder's handling was far superior: Redman found the two models chalk and cheese.

Interested observers at this stage were members of the JWA team, which had been invited to the sessions to carry out driver and tyre testing in anticipation of the coming season. Team boss Wyer was absent, recuperating from a fall that had left him with a broken elbow and the outfit was represented by Manager David Yorke, Engineer John Horsman, Chief Mechanic Ermanno Cuoghi and his assistant Peter Davies. They had brought along a selection of Firestone tyres and Piers Courage to do the initial driving.

Horsman: "the contract wasn't yet in force but everyone was working to that end and we already had mechanics at Porsche learning about the car. We stood around until we were invited to get involved — one car was eventually handed to us. But we couldn't evaluate drivers or tyres as it handled so badly. It went around corners in a series of jerks, like going around the edge of a threepenny bit!"

Having put the Mirage aside Horsman and Co. were starting to wonder what the were letting themselves in for...

Falk and Flegl had recognised for a long while that the 917's aerodynamics weren't correct. The Nurburgring spoiler and the angle at which the flaps were now having to be fixed — vertical — were just two illustrations of that. Flegl: "what sort of engineers would we have been if we hadn't realised that there was an aerodynamic problem?" The question was, how to improve the car without ruining the drag co-efficient. Right from the outset, the order had been to make a car with a very low drag co-efficient, as Falk points out.

Horsman had the rare luxury of a relatively relaxed test, Porsche having to make all the running. Under no pressure, he could enjoy the warm afternoon: "it was beautiful October day, one that brought out clouds of gnats. The windscreen was splattered. Walking around the car I could see that the flaps at the rear hadn't been touched at all by the gnats. It looked as though the air stream was going right over the vertical flaps, leaving them in turbulent air..."

Looking back, Flegl admires the speed with which Horsman diognosed the nature of the complaint: "I was amazed he found out so quickly there was an aerodynamic problem..."

Towards the end of the day Ahrens, driving

33
SPIKES
BonGrip

006, collided with a cat. The oil radiator exploded and the nose was badly damaged. The following day it was repaired by bonding on an alternative nose, one that had been designed to produce greater downforce without tabs (tabs had constantly been knocked askew during the Osterreichring meeting). It featured an air dam prow below the radiator inlet. At the same time the car was converted to settings identical to those of the spyder to allow an honest aerodynamic comparison.

The new nose brought an immediate improvement when running recommenced on the 16th. It worked perfectly, Flegl recalls: "at that moment it was even more obvious that rear downforce was missing".

The major difference in shape between the coupe and the spyder was the latter's flat rear deck. Porsche coupes had always run with a tail that sloped down from the rear wheel axis. Could this time honoured, wind tunnel proven design be at fault?

The answer was close at hand. With the approval of Falk, the JWA lads had been busy modifying the tail of 008 to put a spoiler up into cleaner air. Horsman: "we took an aluminium sheet from the highest point of the wheel arches to continue a line back over the flaps, which provided support for the panel. We put a spoiler up on the back of that".

This impromptu attack on classic Porsche lines was a logical move but at the same time was an unprecedented step away from the low drag creed. It was clearly an anxious time for all concerned. The JWA lads were new boys, keen to make a good impression. Falk and Flegl had seniors to whom to report, and the weight of Porsche doctrine heavy upon their shoulders. However, with all other factors having been made equal, trying a Can Am-type rear deck on the coupe at this juncture was, as Flegl notes, the obvious thing to do.

The makeshift interpretation of the Can Am-style rear deck was fabricated by that master of improvisation, Ermanno Cuoghi. "The idea was to produce a Can Am tail. So we took a big sheet of metal and fixed it with pop rivets and tank tape (a hell of a lot of that)..."

It took Cuoghi and Davies a while to produce it, but it worked. Ahrens reduced his time in 008 from the 1′48″ bracket to the 1′45″ bracket, complaining only of a little understeer. The tail was then transferred to 006 (which had the new nose) and the factory report records the best clocking as 1′45.5″ and Ahrens' comments as: "very good, very stable. Good roadholding and good stability in the turns..."

Redman liked the tail, too. He had gone out with it first and had brought his lap times tumbling. Horsman: "he did three laps without stopping, that was a good sign. Then it was five laps, and so on; he kept on going and the times kept coming down. When he eventually stopped he said, 'that's it, now it's a racing car' ".

The marriage might not yet have been consummated but it was already working extremely well (with a little help from a dead cat and a host of dead gnats).

Piëch refers to the high rear deck as the JWA tail in recognition of the British team's keen anticipation of the key step in the empirical process of making the first powerful Porsche racing car handle. He reflects: "all Porsche coupes up to the Osterreichring had a tail with a rounded rear part. In the wind tunnel the aerodynamics were much better. But previous cars had too little power, with the 917 suddenly we had too much. Aerodynamic stability was suddenly a very important factor. We saw from this modification that this did help much more. Reducing top speed and gaining stability was the right way to go..."

The Porsche hierarchy flew out to see the work of Messrs. Falk, Flegl and Horsman on the 17th; by this time 008 had been equipped with its own improvised air dam nose and Firestone tyres were being run. Times were down further, Ahrens managing 1′43.2″ in 008. Redman's best was 1′43.4″ and he took the spyder, on different tyres, around in 1′41.4″. The most dramatic driver was Kinnunen who had arrived at JWA's behest. He clocked 1′43.7″ in 008, in Flegl's words "driving like hell and throwing the car through the bends, rallying with it!"

Aside from driver and tyre tests, two further modifications were tried on this final day: 006 was run with less camber change to detrimental effect while 008 had its rear panel cut down. This didn't affect lap times but, significantly, did lower the transmission running temperature by 15 degrees centigrade. An open rear would be a feature of the high downforce tail produced by Porsche in the light of the Osterreichring experience.

Weissach saw further pruning of the tail, this time above the engine. Flegl: "here the engine is sucking air down. We thought maybe we could cut the middle out to let the driver see out of the back". Thus was born the classic 917K tail, first seen at Daytona in November '69, during a second test with JWA, this one overseen by Piëch.

Daytona, on account of its banking, was an extremely fast circuit and here the prototype '70 tail was tried alongside the '69 tail, (with the sheet metal modification brought along at Horsman's request). Piëch was left in no doubt: "we decided to have the JWA tail on both cars in January..."

With the Porsche interpretation of the Osterreichring modification performing to everyone's satisfaction JWA's alloy sheet was ditched at Daytona, Horsman fondly recalls.

Meanwhile, over in South Africa the 917 had run its last race of '69 Piper/Attwood having contested November's Kyalami Nine Hours in 010. The car had sported a tidy version of the Osterreichring tail and had won the race (against primarily Chevrolet-Lola opposition) in spite of the crankcase cracking in practice — Piper had been able to weld it with a piece of magnesium wheel!

Scenes from the October Osterreichring test of the 917, showing the tail modification fabricated by Cuoghi and Davies under Horsman's direction, the spyder which inspired it and the air dam nose extension which was grafted onto chassis 008. These photographs were taken and kindly supplied by Davies. Frere's book 'The Racing Porsches' shows a coupe with a makeshift split tail — that was part of the subsequent Weissach development. It can be seen that the original version featured a continuous sheet which obscured the driver's rearward vision. To our knowledge, these are the first photographs of the Cuoghi/Davies modification to have been published.

Seppi's special

The 917 Spyd… produced for Siffert's use i… '69 was a straightforwar… adaption of th… coupe with a … body inspired… the contempor… 908/2 design. … the horizontal… deck with full… width spoiler offering good stability.

As it was airfreighted to the United States during the first week of August 1969, 917 spyder chassis 028 ('917-PA') represented a very traditional approach to what was destined to become an untraditional presence in the highly visible American Can Am championship. This series was in its fourth season and catered for unlimited capacity spyders with no weight restrictions and no concessions to 'road equipment': pukka (two-seater) racing cars with enclosed wheels and awesome power. In years past Porsche simply hadn't had the muscle to be able to consider it.

For Porsche, testing Can Am waters now was a logical move. America represented a majority, not only of the company's export market, of its overall car production. In particular, it had just concluded an agreement with Volkswagen to have VW's U.S. based subsidiary Volkswagen of America act as Porsche importer through a new 'Porsche + Audi' division operating out of its Englewood Cliffs, N.J. headquarters. VW representatives, particularly the company's U.S. competition chief Josef Hoppen, felt strongly that the best means of publicizing this new arrangement was to enter a car in the highly popular Can Am series. The demographics of the championship's audience matched those of the Porsche + Audi division's potential customer base.

Fortunately for Hoppen and his VW colleagues, Porsche now had the 917 programme. While the horsepower of the 4.5 litre flat 12 didn't promise to make it a winner against the 7.0 litre American push-rod stock-block V8s which ruled Can Am, it was felt that a spyder version of the 917 could be sufficiently competitive to accomplish the promotional goals set for the exercise. Further, it would provide valuable experience.

Hoppen: "What we were interested in was exposure for our newly created Porsche + Audi division. Initially what we had in mind was a three year plan which would see Porsche fully competitive by 1971".

The co-operative programme agreed with Porsche for this first year provided for only one 917 to be sent to the States, for Siffert to drive. The initiative came very much from Hoppen and Siffert and the factory did not finance the programme. Flegl explains: "we were not interested in Can Am at this stage. Siffert, however, saw that there was money in it and said, 'just put a McLaren type-body on the 917. I won't have the power but I will try hard...' Siffert bought the car and paid the running costs, and had his own deal with Porsche + Audi".

The car was managed by former Grand Prix driver Richie Ginther who ran a preparation 'shop out of Culver City, California. Steinemann and Flegl would go across to assist only on occasion.

The factory couldn't afford to give the 917-PA

very high priority with so much work on the '69 endurance programme and the car retained much of the coupe's standard specification. Moreover, thanks to the build up to Le Mans, construction of the first spyder, 027, which the factory decided to retain, couldn't begin until the summer and 028 was completed in time for only a brief shakedown on the Weissach skid pan before being sent over for the Mid Ohio race on August 17, round 5 of the 11 round Can Am Challenge Trophy series.

In creating the spyder, the Porsche engineers left the suspension alone and retained standard ATE braking equipment. However, in the interests of saving weight they replaced each iron disc by an iron ring on a titanium bell. They also took the opportunity to increase the width of the 15″ rims to 10.5″ front, 17″ rear, increasing front track slightly and calling for a wider body. The car would run on the same Goodyear tyres as the McLarens.

It was, of course, in the area of aerodynamics that the spyder broke new ground. Not, though, with its nose which (without the provision for headlight assemblies) was just a little more wedge shaped, and did not provide a radiator air outlet. More interesting, from the cockpit back stylist Anatole Lapine's PA body design team followed the general lines that had been created for the later, revised 908/2 spyder. Midway through the season the endurance spyder had been modified with a flatter upper surface from the cockpit back, this a response to the impressive top speed and cornering ability of rival Ferrari and Matra 3.0 litre spyders. In the creation of the PA shape it appears that Lapine simply used his own judgement, not having the benefit of wind tunnel test time. Doubtless he took into account the shape of the established McLaren, Lola and Chaparral Can Am spyders.

The PA lacked aerodynamic devices aside from a low spoiler across the full width of its horizontal rear deck. The tail offered only an upper aerodynamic surface, the lower part being left open behind the wheels — far from the coupe's rounded tail. The overall impression of the PA was of a low, very clean car. There was only a narrow cockpit opening without windscreen surround, while only a simple tubular roll bar and the very top of the engine projected through the flat upper surface.

The simple spyder clothing called for a simplified frame. With less tubing, less bodywork, no windscreen, lighter brakes and no spare wheel the rush-built spyder had to be lighter than the coupe, though at 775 kg. the saving, surprisingly, was far less than 50 kg. Partly because of an extra fuel tank on the righthand side (sitting opposite the oil tank and with its own filler) which increased capacity to 190 litres — the car would have to complete a two hour race non-stop.

The engine and transaxle was familiar 917, with the flat 12 reputedly coaxed to produce 580 b.h.p. in 'sprint' trim. Even so, Siffert was left with around 100 b.h.p. less than the dominant rival Chevrolet-McLaren V8, which carried the best part of 50 kg. less weight thanks to a purpose-designed monocoque chassis. Unless McLaren suffered an uncharacteristic lack of reliability, there was no chance of a Porsche victory. However, strong placings would earn Siffert a lot of dollars, and would give Porsche + Audi the exposure and experience it sought.

Business end of the 917PA spyder. The rear of the frame has been simplified as there is less rear bodywork to carry. Note the extra fuel tank to the right of the engine.

Waving the flag

When Siffert's 917-PA turned up at Mid Ohio the weekend after the Osterreichring endurance finale, it was greeted by an awesome array of more powerful machinery, headed by the Chevrolet-McLaren M8Bs of series pace setters and points leaders Bruce McLaren and Denny Hulme. In typical fashion the Colnbrook, England based team took first and second places, Hulme pulling away to win, while McLaren took second in spite of an oil pump failure 17 miles from the chequered flag. Siffert found the PA far more controllable than the coupe he disliked, if short of elephant-engine type grunt. He collected a credible fourth place a lap down, in spite of having to cope with a balky gear shift linkage.

That problem continued to haunt the PA effort at Road America. It caused the Swiss to miss a shift, forcing retirement. Here the car ran a front spoiler and front tabs. By Bridgehampton, scene of the third appearance, Ginther's men had revised the linkage and had converted the gearbox to four speeds, helping combat the problem. The once clean lines of the car were now further marred by an extension to the rear spoiler. In addition, the car had front wheel arch air vents and also side louvres, as seen on the coupes in Austria, while rear brake cooling inlets were set into the rear deck. Siffert was still not able to challenge the McLarens but there were only a couple of other Chevrolet engined cars well enough prepared and well enough driven to worry him and on this occasion he finished third and on the same lap, his best showing so far (the McLarens as usual filling the top two places).

From New York's Long Island the Can Am circus trekked back across country to Michigan International Speedway outside of Detroit where Siffert brought 028 home fourth, in spite of a lifeless cooling fan. The drive gears had failed, leaving Siffert to gently ease the car home behind three works McLarens (Gurney driving a spare car

Siffert hustles pretty 91 around attractive R America circ Note the s front tabs spoiler extensio searc downfc

When Siffert arrived on the Am scene the p makers were th works Chevrole McLarens of Hulme (no. 5) McLaren (no. 4 Note the team's high wings whi followed Form One practice.

Siffert in full at Michigan, he collected f place. Note th front and rear tabs. Photo: Ludvigsen.

on this occasion).

Laguna Seca in California followed (soon after that Osterreichring test at which the sister car had played an important role) and saw Siffert finish a rather disappointing fifth in yet another McLaren-dominated race. Here the car was running a (split) oil radiator air exit and very large front tabs, one of which had been damaged by another competitor on the warm up lap, leaving Siffert with an uncomfortable amount of understeer.

Then came Riverside, further south in California, and a modified nose shape — chisel-like, it was less curvacious with flatter sides and a flatter slope behind its pointed leading edge. It sported prominent side fences and a prominent spoiler across the front of an undivided radiator air exit. NACA ducts collected air for both brakes and driver. Produced by Ginther's crew, it was designed to offer maximum front end downforce without the need for large tabs. Alas, in the race Siffert was black flagged for excessive oil loss, though he still couldn't get near those orange cars...

The final Can Am race was held at Texas International Speedway early in November and here Siffert put in a solid performance for fifth while McLaren won the title after Hulme's engine blew as he was headed for the honour. Overall Siffert finished fourth in spite of missing four early rounds, and scooped over $50,000 dollars for his efforts.

Riverside saw 917PA sport modified, wee shaped nose. clothing is no quite a contra the smooth-lo style that had shipped to the three months earlier.

70

The numbers game

"JWA was a small team", Chief Mechanic Ermanno Cuoghi points out, "with only one engineer (Horsman) and around 15 persons. That wasn't much for a team doing 24 hour races — nowadays, in the Eighties, we have at least 25 persons for 1½ hour (Formula One) races..."

With Gulf support JWA had won the 1968 World Championship and Le Mans in 1968 and in 1969 but by 1969 it had become obvious that the GT40 programme was living on borrowed time. And equally as obvious that a 3.0 litre prototype, such as JWA had under development, would stand little chance in the long term against the new breed of 5.0 litre prototype. Wyer had flown promptly to Stuttgart in response to Steinemann's initial inquiry.

The essential points of the subsequent agreement were that Porsche would withdraw from World Championship participation at the end of '69 and that it would loan JWA seven cars and would provide all parts for their preparation free of charge. Further, it would continue development of the model and make available to JWA all improvements in specification immediately, and before general release to 917 customers. JWA was to run two cars, except at Le Mans where a third would be added, and its operational costs were to be borne by Gulf. It was to have complete operational freedom.

The agreement was formalized in a two year contract, signed just before the Osterreichring 1000 km. race, to take effect as from the start of 1970. It provided for chassis to be built in Germany but prepared at JWA's Slough, England base, whereas engines were to be returned to Piëch's Experimental Department for preparation by a team headed by engine development specialist Paul Hensler. The cars would run on Firestone tyres, as per JWA's existing contract.

Porsche further loaned JWA three 911 road cars and a workshop transporter. Two of the drivers were to be employed by Porsche, two by JWA. The former nominated Siffert and Redman. For the latter, JWA chose Rodriguez and a successful Finnish Porsche 908/2 privateer and Formula Three driver, Leo Kinnunen. Ickx would have been its first choice to partner the Mexican Grand Prix driver but he had moved to Ferrari.

The marriage between Porsche and JWA gave Piech weapons and soldiers well capable of securing that elusive Le Mans win. But Piech had learnt that there is one other major factor to consider in respect of Le Mans success: numbers. He had come to the conclusion that, even in a competitive three car team, one car would retire through driver error and one car would retire through technical problems, leaving one car which could win if, and only if, it didn't suffer serious setbacks: "In a battle like Le Mans the number of warships also counted..."

Ferrari was preparing its own 25-off, 5.0 litre prototype for 1970 and had powerful allies, in particular the experienced Filipinetti and NART operations. Both had placed orders for 5.0 litre cars to run alongside the works team, which was to be expanded to three or more cars for 1970. That coveted Le Mans win was no forgone conclusion, even with JWA's help.

Piëch reckoned he would have to be able to count upon at least two cars being around at the finish to have a realistic chance of beating Ferrari: that meant fielding six competitive 917s. Having no existing back up team (such as a Filipinetti or a NART) capable of providing substantial support it was necessary for Porsche to create one. Consequently, while on the technical front JWA would indisputably be number one (as per the contract), over the season Porsche would help nurture a second 917 team.

It was considered important that the back-up team should contest the entire season, rather than two or three events, Piëch explains, if it was to learn enough to get it right on the day. Finance for the programme came from the Salzburg-based Porsche Konstrukionen K.G., the Austrian Porsche distributorship owned by the Piech family. The Porsche Salzburg team drew heavily upon the factory's customer service department (as all Porsche 917 customers were entitled to do) for the preparation and running of its cars. It signed a tyre contract with Goodyear.

Porsche Salzburg employed the strong driver pairings of Elford/Ahrens and Herrmann/Attwood, providing continuing employment for these well established, Porsche-contracted drivers. At races it was stongly assisted by key Porsche personnel, in accordance with its pupil status.

There wasn't much that Porsche could teach JWA about winning races. While the English team had its operational freedom (with Flegl handing over race engineering to Horsman), Falk and Flegl were assigned to accompany JWA to races and test sessions, to maintain the closest possible technical co-operation. Piech would also continue to attend races, to oversee technical progress, while back at base he assigned engineers to develop a revised long tail version of the 917 specifically for Le Mans. That 24 hour race counted above all else.

Previous pa
colour -
Italian at M
Giunti's F
leads the
chas
Rodrigue
Siffert. Rodr
came throu
win this eve
he had at Da
(i

50 b.h.p. from thin air

Piper's cracked crankcase at Kyalami hadn't been an isolated incident. The engine was inclined to develop cracks running from the holes providing access to the scavenge pick up filters, Mezger admits. Consequently, the bottom end was redesigned for 1970 with pick ups suspended above a closed crankcase floor. Another weakness had revealed itself on the Can Am car — the gears driving the blower had not been sufficiently well cushioned, and this was attended to with a rubber drive coupling. There was also a very slight oil leak at the camshaft drive which wasn't a problem in racing terms (but would have been unacceptable for a production engine, Piëch notes). This would be cured with the bigger capacity engine now under development, in the face of the threat from the 5.0 litre Ferrari. Already (in November '69) Porsche had applied for homologation of its alternative crankshaft.

Over the course of 1969, investigations had been made into three-piece crankshafts, following a difficulty in the machining of the one-piece case-hardened item. The challenge was to find a satisfactory method of attaching the crank halves (having induction hardened journals) to the case-hardened central pinion. A glued shaft worked well until the engine got hot, while an electron-beam welded shaft similarly proved unreliable. The problem here was with the weld seam, due to the employment of two different steels. Mezger says that he was advised to develop a method of using a nickel plate between the two steels: this was time consuming and in any case it was found that the one-piece shaft worked perfectly well, even if it could not be ground as had been originally specified.

By January 1970 power was in the region of 565 b.h.p. at 8,400 r.p.m. and the engine was proven as remarkably free of mechanical problems. However, during its first season it had acquired a reputation as easy to over-rev: there being no suitable rev-limiter, drivers who were not accustomed to powerful engines had, somewhat inevitably, found it challenging. In retrospect, both Piëch and Mezger stress that a 1000 r.p.m. safety margin was reasonable — it was a question of certain drivers having to adapt. Piëch: "with such a powerful car little mistakes are less forgiven..."

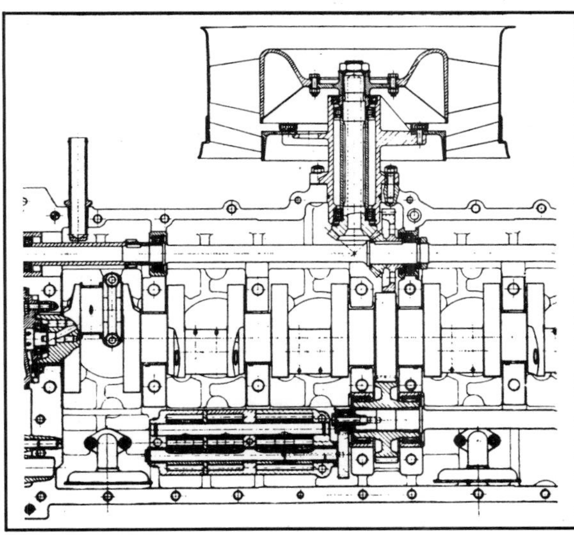

ongitudinal of the 1970 ine showing venge pick-s have been ted above a d crankcase r (Porsche).

The 917 was also reputed to have a difficult driving position, and to suffer from too much chassis flex. At the time the forward driving position was unique, and was reminiscent of the difficult-to-control pre-war Auto Union Grand Prix car. Race reports made comments such as:

otype of the 7 Kurz body uced for the 1970 season (Porsche).

f, in colour: *icing at —but Amon errari is a lap Rodriguez' 917 due to setbacks fast Italian*

Shell
3
SHELL
7
Gulf-Porsche
7
Gulf

"the driver has little feel of what the back end of the car is doing until it has done it", and some reports suggested that the chassis was twisting to the detriment of road holding. Certainly, in its original form the car was difficult to drive. In his book 'Porsche — Excellence was Expected' (ISBN 0 915 038 099), Karl Ludvigsen reminds us that Mitter, before he had been killed in a single seater at the Nurburgring, had nicknamed it 'The Ulcer' and that Herrmann was later quoted as recalling that "for a long time the 917 remained 'unexplored territory' that held more and more surprises in wait for me. It was often mischievous and played tricks like a stubborn horse". However, now that the aerodynamic problem had been solved the car was far more civilized, giving lie to those ill-informed press reports which had faulted driving position or chassis rigidity.

In fact the chassis had been stiffened following the routine 1000 km. pave test, which had taken place in the autumn of '69, but the increase in rigidity was very slight, and certainly not significant, according to Flegl. It was a question of improving durability rather than torsional rigidity, which (as with earlier cars) had not been found a problem in terms of handling. In fact, from the outset the 917 spaceframe had been reckoned to be stiffer than that of the 908. In the early days there had sometimes been a problem with the gear linkage due to give in the frame and this and cracks that showed up over the course of the pave test were tackled by the slightly revised frame with simplified support for the 1970 Kurz tail, which only provided an upper aerodynamic surface.

With the revised 917K chassis there were slight suspension revisions and henceforth wider (initially 10.5″ front, 15″ rear) rims would be run, with zero camber at the front and a small degree of positive camber at the rear.

The 1970 car ran without side exhausts: each trio of cylinders merged into a pipe which in turn merged into a single, rear exit megaphone for the respective bank. With very limited space under the engine, keeping the pipes of equal length from cylinder to first merging point had caused a headache, Piëch recalls. In the end models made from accordion-folded paper tube had been coated with epoxy to produce a mould, and some very skilled iron mastery had been employed to produce the final product. Thanks to the revised system, first tried at the late '69 Osterreichring test, and the open rear end, Porsche could dispense with the water cooled driving suit! The new exhaust system also reduced cockpit noise to a more tolerable level and overcame the problem of fuel system overheating. Also significant was the fact that the engine bay temperature reduction provided by the re-routed exhaust, and in particular the open rear end was "a major improvement for durability", according to Piëch.

Transmission heat dissipation was further enhanced, and transaxle strength was improved by a stronger transaxle casing with new ribbing and cast-in oil lines rather than external ones (as had failed on the Le Mans spyder). Generally four speeds would be utilized (reflecting the vast torque available) and a failsafe was incorporated in the gate: first could only be selected if a concentric ring around the lever was lifted, otherwise pushing the lever forward from second selected third.

Brake development had seen the titanium bell on the PA replaced by a more satisfactory aluminium alternative and this was taken a stage further by a rear disc with bell and internal cooling vanes produced as a single, highly complex aluminium casting, to which copper chrome alloy rings were riveted. Air was fed into the perimeter of the disc and was extracted by vanes on the bell. Pistons were now aluminium and were inverted in the caliper so as to keep the fluid further from the hot pads, to leave an air cavity near the pad, and to minimize the contact surface between piston and back plate. In reducing heat transfer between piston and back plate (which had intensified the fluid heating problem) this solution cut out the automatic wear adjustment mechanism.

The 917K body productionized for 1970 was approximately the same length as the original Kurz but was significantly lighter thanks to its open rear, and the use of a P.V.C. foam sandwich which provided the greater rigidity called for by a flat rear deck. Where previously there had been a single sheet of 5 mm. thick g.r.p. there would now be a 4 mm. thick foam layer sandwiched between 2 mm. thick g.r.p. sheets: thicker but a little lighter and substantially more rigid. The overall weight saving was in the region of 15 kg.

The new shape offered a blunt nose with an air dam below the radiator inlet and a wide, undivided radiator air exit (across the front of which was an air deflector lip). The car's waistline was higher and led into a gently upswept ramp either side of the engine. At the end of each ramp was an adjustable spoiler. The tail was left open above the engine but a horizontal panel ran back from the engine's air duct roofing, extending the central valley floor from the rear cockpit window to the end of the tail. The valley was left unobstructed in the interests of rearward vision.

The new look nose (as seen at the Osterreichring test) incorporated a reshaped front air intake (internally split) serving both brakes and radiator. Above, either side of the nose were NACA ducts to collect cockpit cooling air while NACA ducts set into the tail ramps collected transmission cooling air. Front wheel arch extractor vents were carried over from the late '69 car.

Homologated as an evolution of the original car, the new body was a little wider to accept the wider rims and overall the frontal area was up by 10%, while the drag co-efficient had worsened from 0.4 to 0.464. The net result was a gain in cornering performance which, at a circuit such as the Osterreichring, Mezger compared to a 50 b.h.p. jump in engine output. However, Piëch was not content with the co-efficient of drag as it now stood...

Fiat picks up the gauntlet

Its aerodynamic problem overcome, the 917 set a standard of performance that left American-engined homologated sports cars and 3.0 litre-engined prototypes struggling. Only the lightweight 3.0 litre runners had any hope, on slow, sinuous circuits. For the special case of the Targa Florio, and perhaps the Nurburgring, Porsche developed a new version of its flyweight 908 spyder with lower moment of polar inertia for even greater agility. Elsewhere the 917 was the weapon, and only one company came forward with the resources to challenge it. That company was Fiat.

Fiat acquired a 50% stake in Ferrari in mid '69 and immediately the Maranello marque could begin preparation of its own 25-off prototype. The 512S was rush-produced by Mauro Forghieri's race engineering team within five months and consequently drew heavily upon existing Ferrari technology. Its engine was derived from a '68/'69 7.0 litre Can Am power plant, which in turn was a derivative of the marque's mid Sixties twin cam, two valve 60 degree V12 prototype power plant. By this stage Ferrari was employing four valve heads, however. The block was cast in aluminium, in one piece with the crankcase and carried cast iron liners. The crankshaft ran in seven plain bearings and had six pins. It drove the camshafts via chains.

A single plug per cylinder was fired by a Marelli transistorized ignition system, while fuel was supplied by a Lucas injection system. The four valves were set at an included angle of 25 degrees and the piston crown was slightly convex. On an 11.0:1 compression ratio, the 512 engine produced a claimed 550 b.h.p. at 8,500 r.p.m. from a full 5.0 litre capacity, (87.0 mm. x 70.0 mm.) — before extensive development work had been undertaken. With the first race at the end of January, Forghieri's team didn't have time on its side.

The Ferrari 512 chassis was a coupe-bodied derivative of the familiar '69 spyder running on a 2400 mm. wheelbase with 15″ rims, 11″ wide at the front, 16″ at the rear. Oil radiators were mounted in the nose (one either side of the spare wheel), water radiators in a mid position, (one either side of the engine). The centrally plated spaceframe extended upwards to carry the windscreen and roof and rearwards to carry the semi (circa 70%) stressed drivetrain. The gearbox was Ferrari's own five-speed unit, derived, like the engine, from the mid Sixties P4 prototype. The Girling brakes, like the conventional outboard-type suspension, followed contemporary Ferrari Formula One practice.

The 512 body broke no new ground and included a high rear deck, with slatted window concealing the engine. The obvious drawbacks of the rush-designed and built newcomer were its weight, which was quoted as 880 kg., and its lack of development time. There hadn't been enough time to produce exotic lightweight parts and testing hadn't been able to get underway until November of '69...

heart of the 512S was a degree V12 ed from the que's classic mid-Sixties ortscar unit. However, it ed 48 rather n 24 valves.

f, in colour: rsus its ivals of e works team and burg team. ez leads Spa (left) ffert leads at the chring. on six of ces with the ving one or the rival

20
25

21
73
Gulf

Making of a legend

As we have seen, the build up to the opening round of the 1970 World Championship for Makes, the Daytona 24 Hours on January 31/February 1, had begun the previous November with a major Porsche 917 test at the Speedway. The track had been hired for a week by Gulf and the exercise had culminated in a successful 26 hour endurance run. The chassis on hand had been 011 and 012, and in addition to Siffert, drivers had included Rodriguez and Hobbs. Rodriguez had suffered the ignominy of crashing heavily early in the week, his car caught by a gust of wind on the banking, while Hobbs had been unlucky enough to miss a gear, wrecking an engine. That hadn't endeared him to Porsche and had helped pave Kinnunen's path to the drive alongside Rodriguez.

Early in January news came from Daytona of Ferrari pre-race testing. Andretti had found the new 512S: "...very impressive. It felt very correct, aerodynamically and mechanically...It was heavy but very well balanced", as he later related to the author. His times were only a second off the 917's November pace.

At this late stage JWA received the remaining two of the three 917s it would run in the 24 hour race. All three cars had a D-shaped window set into the roof above the windscreen to allow the driver to see further ahead on the banking — an important consideration with lots of cars at least 50 m.p.h. slower.

While the lads at Slough prepared for the upcoming marathon, Siffert broke his foot in a silly karting accident and Redman gave the new tail its race debut, on Piper's car in the non-championship Buenos Aires 1000 km. race. Against 3.0 litre opposition, including works cars from Matra and Alfa Romeo, Redman dominated practice and the first 22 laps of the autodrome, then he was struck by the first of a series of tyre failures. The car was eventually withdrawn following a collision. Piper was still using the '69 nose and 9" fronts and the tyre failures were attributed to the negative camber that had been run to combat understeer.

The 917 came close to having only 3.0 litre prototype opposition at Daytona: the 512's 25-off run was running late and homologation was granted just in the nick of time. Cuoghi recalls the Ferrari lads "flew out with the cargo, arriving cold and miserable, and tired out". Advantage JWA.

The 917s required stiffer springs to resist the high 'g' forces on the banking while transparent plastic film as used to protect helicopter blades was put on the nose to help resist the inevitable blasting from the notorious Daytona shell particles. The concours turn out of the 917s in Gulf livery drew widespread praise.

In addition to the three JWA cars, there was a lone 917 in Porsche Salzburg colours for Elford/Ahrens. This was an ex-November test car (011) on loan from Porsche pending delivery of the team's own cars. In his autobiography 'The

Porsche prod[...] new rear bra[...] Daytona with[...] vanes betwee[...] copper faces, [...] vanes in one [...] with the bell. [...] caliper is still [...] ATE four pis[...] item.

WA 917 of ...rt/Redman ...ame clutch ...o complete ... 1, 2 in the ...ng event of ...). Note the ...t of taping ...at has been ...ary to hold ...e together.

Certain Sound' (ISBN 2 88001 111 6), Wyer records his concern at the amount of factory attention this car was getting, given that "...it was clearly understood that we would be competing against privately owned 917s".

Having retired from a 200 mile event held at Buenos Aires the weekend following the 1000 km. race due to gear linkage failure, less than two weeks later Piper's 010 chassis turned up, to be driven by Dean and Gregg. The story goes that they had found it in a Miami freight shed in transit from Argentina to London, while searching for their own 908!

Opposition to Porsche was headed by three works cars from Maranello, supported by two private entries, one of them from NART. Best of the rest was a pair of works Matra Group 6 cars.

Ferrari was to be taken seriously, though preparation paled in comparison to that of JWA. Horsman: "it was the first time I had seen the 512. It did look a bit cobbled up, a bit Alfa Romeo-ish..." Andretti agrees that the 917K was the more sophisticated car, recalling that "it looked formidable. Top speed, braking, acceleration, the 917 was better..."

Nevertheless, in untimed practice on Wednesday and Thursday Andretti set the fastest lap, chased by Siffert, who couldn't brake as hard as he would have liked thanks to having his foot in plaster. Looking on, *Sport Auto* Editor Gerard 'Jabby' Crombac reckoned that the new 512 gained in handling over the 917, agreeing that the lighter Porsche was winning on acceleration.

Official practice was wet and it came down to bravery on the banking. Andretti took pole by 1.3 seconds from Siffert with Rodriguez third, Elford fourth, Ickx fifth and Gurney (NART) sixth. These six Grand Prix rank drivers were, with Redman, the only ones able to exploit the full potential of the 5.0 litre prototypes, Crombac noting that the new generation 'Supercars' called for 'Superdrivers'...

The Piper car failed to survive practice, a camshaft seizing.

After the battles of the preceding week the race was rather an anti climax. Andretti chased hard for three quarters of an hour, then needed fuel: the 512 had a consumption problem. Already Ickx had suffered a loose wheel, and Ferrari fortunes would only get worse. The race was Porsche's from start to finish, without a serious challenge from the 45 minute mark. Siffert/Redman led the first three hours then struck problems, leaving Rodriguez/Kinnunen to win. Elford/Ahrens suffered a front brake problem early on, later their lights failed, then a shock absorber broke and finally a tyre let go and Ahrens had to drive a lap on the flat, wearing a hole in the fuel tank, which ended the run under the cover of darkness.

Meanwhile, Siffert/Redman's initial setback, a puncture caused by a piece of shell which in turn had ripped out a brake hose, had been followed by overnight ignition problems and a broken shock absorber. The best part of 20 laps had been lost

20
Shell
20

and then Sunday morning brought clutch failure at 7.00 am. Cuoghi: "we were pushing the car away when a Porsche engineer said, 'you can change the clutch, it should only take 20 minutes'. The problem was that we lacked practical experience of undertaking jobs such as that during a race. We had already pushed the car out of the first gate to the truck so we pushed it back in through a second gate, and were off again..."

Sure enough, in spite of having fallen almost 50 laps behind, Siffert and Redman were still in third place. And two chassis failures on the delayed Andretti/Merzario/Ickx 512S brought second to within grasp with some flat out motoring. The Ferrari was eventually overhauled with only two laps left to run...

The winning car's run had only been bothered by a broken exhaust and the g.r.p. bodywork not standing up well to the hammering. Peter Davies recalls that both cars were "virtually wrecked after the race; the body had been eaten away and had needed a lot of taping to survive".

After the race the cars were taken to the Gulf Research Centre in Pittsburgh, in which two bays had been set aside for the team to prepare for Sebring in late March. One new car was flown out from the UK as a race car, its sister to be the Daytona spare. During this period the JWA lads made a number of modifications to the cars, including the fitting of a new, 120 litre fuel tank in accordance with a C.S.I. ruling. Porsche arranged for a single fuel tank to be carried on the righthand side in an aluminium sponson and fed via a vertical filler which emerged through the tail, just aft of the driver's door. The tank itself was a flexible, foam filled saftey bag and 120 litres provided sufficient for 50 — 55 minutes running. Putting all the fuel on the righthand side dispensed with the need for the cross-cockpit fuel line which had worried some drivers.

JWA installed its own British made Graviner aircraft-type central fire extinguisher system. This had a bottle in the rear of a cockpit and spray lines through the cockpit and across the fuel tank and the inlet trumpets. Some Bosch items were replaced by Lucas parts and the nose was reinforced with carbon fibre rope, and alloy sheet stoneguards were fitted under the wheel arches. Oil was routed via hoses rather than the chassis tubes, helping to reduce cockpit temperature.

Better cockpit cooling was provided via a third, central NACA duct just ahead of the windscreen, while an air outlet set into the roof ensured proper through ventilation, really making the cooling provisions work. Cooling was also provided for the rear brakes, via trunking from NACA ducts set into either side of the tail, where the ramp flared up to meet the central valley walls. The wheel arches were widened slightly to accommodate a wider rim option. The modified JWA cars weighed 812 kg. dry.

At the end of February a couple of days were spent testing at Sebring in anticipation of the 12 hour race. Horsman recalls: "walking down the pit lane, I noticed a trail of solder. I followed it up and it stopped at the rear wheels of our car. The alloy vanes were melting between the copper faces!" Lighter on brakes, Daytona had been kind to Porsche. Henceforth iron discs would be used front and rear. However, Porsche had another brake-related development for Sebring, an alternative front upright and stub axle assembly.

With the pistons reversed in the calipers, pad knock-off had been proving a problem: drivers had frequently needed to pump the pedal at Daytona. There had also been taper wear on the pads and both problems were blamed on wobbling of the front discs caused by flexing of the stub axle or play in the bearings. Porsche's prompt response was a 'live' stub axle. Whereas previously the wheel hub had run on taper roller bearings about a fixed stub axle, now the hub was attached to a stub axle which rotated within the upright. The new live axle ran in large taper roller bearings set into the upright, in the manner of the rear axle arrangement, and was retained at its inner end against the inner bearing race by a flange. The flange was secured by four studs.

The design looked sound (as was to be expected from Porsche) and it ran troublefree for four hours on 015 with Redman at the controls. It didn't cure the problem of taper wear but it did overcome pad knock-off. It would be used (exclusively) by JWA in the upcoming 12 hour race, subject to the successful outcome of an endurance test at Weissach.

Another development tried at Sebring was an ABS anti-lock braking system, but this testing was of an experimental nature: it wasn't felt that the system was reliable enough yet.

Back in Europe, the Salzburg Daytona car (011) was taken from the factory down to Sicily for the annual pre-race Targa Florio testing. However, as it was felt that the 917 was essentially too big and too heavy for the hillclimb-like course, the agile 908/3 model that had been developed specifically for the race was the focus of attention. And sadly the 917 was wrecked by an engineer who collided with a truck on a bridge. Flegl: "there wasn't enough room left on the bridge and the truck tore the car apart. The truck wasn't going very carefully, but the engineer should have taken more care".

Meanwhile, in Florida the cars were turned out for Sebring with 17" wide rear rims, Borg & Beck clutches and a titanium output shaft. In addition to the wider rear rims JWA now had a 12" front rim option, but this had been found to make the car unstable under heavy braking. The Borg & Beck clutch had sintered metal linings and wore less rapidly, having less affect on clearance. The titanium replacement for the power output layshaft was 24 mm. in diameter and weighed 1.02 kg. as against 1.585 kg. for the 22 mm. steel original.

Salzburg flew out two cars, which were painted in Porsche-Audi USA colours, to be driven by Elford/Ahrens and Herrmann/Lins (the latter on

song for the burg team at sterreichring memorable, rens/Marko red) leading ntil the tank ran dry. rtheless, the had won the that counted t, Le Mans.

a one-off basis). Heading the opposition were three works 512s, two of which were in 'spyder' trim, with the roof panel and engine cover removed to allow air to flow under a wide, carefully profiled 'aerodynamic' roll bar. This worked in conjunction with a reshaped deck that sported bigger rear spoilers, while the lower part of the tail was cutaway behind the rear wheels. Weight was 855 kg. dry and Andretti found the model more agile than the coupe. Ferrari V12 power was now certainly a match for Porsche V12 power and fuel consumption had been improved.

Siffert set the early qualifying pace but while his car was undergoing race preparation Andretti continued working his times down to claim another pole position. Elford was third fastest, while works 3.0 litre teams from Matra and Alfa Romeo were rather overshadowed: the only other team in the hunt was NART, with its 512S coupe.

Early on race morning Flegl was called from Germany to be advised that the Weissach endurance test of the new front hub had continued beyond the scheduled 18 hours, and that the hub had eventually failed: the design was suspect. In his autobiography Wyer recalls: "Flegl emphasized that the decision as to whether or not to change the hubs had been left to me. They still believed that the new design would survive 12 hours at Sebring but obviously there must now be an element of doubt. It was a moment of extreme truth and whatever I did was likely to be wrong. The race started at 10.00 am. and the cars were already being warmed up in the garage before going out on the track. To start tearing them apart at such a time would be to invite mistakes..."

Andretti led from the rolling start to the first round of pit stops, at which slicker Porsche pit work left the three fast 917s out in front. However, Andretti and Ickx were looking strong in the 512 spyders and they moved up to first and second as JWA suffered a puncture (Rodriguez) and a loose ignition wire (Redman), then Elford collided with a 911, after it and a Lancia had carelessly contrived to stray in front of him. "It took the left rear corner off..." A great shame: "the car had been going well and I had been having a great fight with Siffert..."

Even at this early stage the other Salzburg car was also out, its engine over-revved. And just under the three hour mark the Siffert/Redman car came in with only the upright and the inner half of the caliper remaining on the left front. The retaining studs had failed, leaving only the caliper to hold the wheel on! An upright assembly had to be taken from the spare car, the stop costing half and hour. The mechanics then started building up other complete upright assemblies, just in case...

When the Rodriguez/Kinnunen car suffered the same failure on the more heavily loaded left side only 15 minutes were lost. Alas, Kinnunen then collided with a Mustang, wasting more time. The damage wasn't too severe, and the tail was patched up with a rather novel new crossbeam: a Sebring fence post! More trouble was in store for Siffert/Redman. Cuoghi: "the fan retaining bolts broke in front of us and the fan flew over the grandstand!"

At half distance Ferrari lay one — two — three. Siffert joined Rodriguez, while Redman got going again only to suffer another broken stub axle. The car was withdrawn to leave adequate spares for the other runner.

Late in the race both Ferrari spyders broke. With the coupe having been badly delayed, this left Rodriguez/Siffert in a comfortable lead. Alas, the right front hub failed with less than 20 minutes to run. The car was coaxed home fourth while the Ferrari coupe evened the score.

A post-race examination of the titanium power shaft showed greater permanent deformation than steel so that type was reinstated. Revised live axles were given high priority, but could not be readied in time for Brands Hatch in mid April so the drivers had to live with pad knock-off for a little while longer.

Brands Hatch saw Elford partnered by Hulme

Elford/Ahrens went well in t... early stages o... Sebring 12 ho... only to be eliminated by collision with backmarker. ... not been thus sidelined, the serious delays which befell t... other front ru... might well ha... presented it w... easy victory.

WA Sebring the story of ont upright. 'uoghi tends e Rodriguez ich finished th after two ıge failures.

as Ahrens had been injured testing a new *Langheck*, while Herrmann was joined by Attwood. Ferrari's deal with Andretti only extended to North America and it ran just two spyders, for Ickx and Amon. Matra and Alfa Romeo tried again, but even on this tight circuit were overshadowed. Elford was the fastest 917 driver in qualifying, but the Ferraris were faster still.

Rodriguez only started from the third row and early in the race, which had been wet from the word go, he missed a yellow flag while making up places through the spray. Upon the instructions of Clerk of the Course Nick Syrett he was brought into his pit where Syrett read him the riot act. Then, as Davies aptly put it: "the red haze took over..."

By lap 20 Rodriguez was in the lead, and speedboating away from the early lead battle between Elford and Amon. Cuoghi reminds us, "the car had so much power that to keep control in the wet was not an easy job — the cars were spinning very often", and certainly even Rodriguez had a couple of spins on his epic drive. He drove until just before the maximum permissible three and a half hour mark, then surrendered his car to Kinnunen for only one stint, on a drying track.

At this stage Siffert/Redman, who had suffered a puncture during the opening laps, were two laps down. Siffert was able to draw in Kinnunen at around half a second a lap, then Redman took over only to crash at Westfield. That left the Salzburg cars to claim second and third, both Ferraris having suffered setbacks, although the second Austrian car was lucky to beat a Matra and Amon's recovering 512.

Elford went well, driving most of the race as Hulme hated the 917 in the wet. He recalls surviving a "monster spin" at Clearways and admits, "I thought I was pretty good in the rain but that day there was no way to do anything about Rodriguez".

Brands Hatch clashed with the Le Mans test weekend and Redman had flown over with Wyer and Horsman on Saturday but it had rained most of the time. The British driver had tried a 917 in '69 long tail trim, then '70 K trim, in which guise he had felt confident enough to set fastest time overall at 3′33.5″, more than six seconds off Elford's lap record. Shortly afterwards the same test car (008) was taken by the factory to the Nurburgring to try an important new development on the South Loop: the long awaited 5.0 litre engine.

In fact engine Project 912/10 was of 4907 cc. capacity, with the new crankshaft giving a 4.4 mm. longer stroke and the bore enlarged by 1 mm. (to produce 86 x 70.4mm). There were no other significant modifications, Mezger confirms, yet power was now over 580 b.h.p. at 8,400 r.p.m. Equally important was a 10% more torque at 6,400 r.p.m. (and almost as much all the way from 5000 r.p.m.). In 'The Racing Porsches' (ISBN 0 668 02972 2) Paul Frere notes that for Monza the cars were geared so as to drop from maximum revs in third to 6,400 in fourth giving tremendous acceleration from the circuit's fast corners.

Braking was another improvement for the Italian race thanks to a satisfactory live axle and a switch to Girling brakes. The axle was now retained by a single central bolt. Girling discs and four pot calipers had been run by JWA on the GT40 but had been denied to Porsche-entered cars due to trade patent agreements. JWA asked for permission to run them on the 917. Horsman: "we didn't like the look of the ATE brakes and went back to something we knew". The British calipers had larger pistons on the abutment side than on the trailing side to combat taper wear and the drivers found a harder pedal. They were run with Ferodo pads.

Salzburg had to stick with ATE brakes and could not yet race the 4.9 engine, in accordance with the JWA contract. Ahrens was back in the team and there were three other 917s, from Piper

Rodriguez an Elford go wa. At Brands H. was so wet th anyone could excused spinn 917 . . . (Gul archive).

ıff of which ls are made: ıez, Porsche rands Hatch 1970. (Gulf archive).

(whose car had been entered for Brands Hatch but again hadn't survived practice), AAW and Gesipa Rivets. Ferrari countered with three works cars (one of which was a spyder) and was supported by two private entries (one of which was the Filipinetti car). Ickx was absent due to injury and consequently Surtees joined the team. Matra and Alfa Romeo gave vain chase.

Siffert found he could take the Parabolica in third thanks to the torque of the 4.9 litre engine and claimed pole just 0.01 second off the Grand Prix lap record. However, the new engine had suffered a minor oil leak. Wyer didn't feel the 4.9 engine was necessary to beat Ferrari, Piëch did. Consequently, with JWA refusing to race it, Elford was given the pleasure. "It was nice to be given a little extra power against people like Siffert and Rodriguez. It had been very hard work before; it made life a little easier".

After a busy opening phase, Elford used the torque of the 4.9 engine to go clear of Rodriguez and the Ferraris (headed by Giunti in the spyder) while Siffert limped to the pits, having spun in the Lesmo corners dodging a backmarker and damaged the right rear corner. Elford and Ahrens looked a good bet for victory, if not by a great margin, when just after half distance Elford had a fright. "A rear tyre went bang and I went backwards into the guard rail..."

That left Kinnunen, on his only stint, in front with Giunti not far behind, and closing. Superior pit work gave Rodriguez the length of the straight over the spyder and he was able to slowly but surely build a cushion. Consequently Amon was transferred from a coupe to the well placed spyder. Had this tactic been implemented earlier, and had Amon not suffered a flash fire as he tried to take up the chase, the finish alongside Rodriguez might well have been a bid for victory, rather than the honour of finishing on the same lap...

Siffert/Redman finished a lowly 12th after lengthy repairs, while the AAW and Gesipa Rivets cars similarly came in behind the outpaced Group 6 class winners. Salzburg's second car lost its engine and Piper lost gear selection.

The next race was the Targa Florio, for which the factory prepared a team of 908/3s. However, a 917 was entered by Salzburg and Elford took it around in 35′06.6″, as against 34′10.0″ for Siffert's fastest 908 and 34′46.0″ for Vaccarella in a 512S spyder. "I came back after one lap and almost had to be dragged from the car, I was so washed out! Mainly from nervous exhaustion — I was on the edge all the way...

"Visibility was difficult due to the size of the car. It was so big that it needed twice as much attention". Elford attributes his time to the car's fabulous torque — he only used first and second gear most of the way.

Between qualifying and the race Porsche negotiated with JWA for Salzburg to run a 908/3, so Elford had a more practical car for the race: "there is no way I could have driven the 917 two or three laps..."

After the Sicilian classic (won by Siffert/Redman) came the high speed blind around the public roads at Francorchamps. While JWA hadn't found much to criticise mechanically, it did feel that it could help further improve the 917's aerodynamics and the first fruit of this was seen at Spa. Horsman explains: "you need high downforce at Spa. With 150 m.p.h. corners you want the car glued to the road". Consequently, an aluminium panel was inserted in the valley behind the engine to sweep the valley floor upwards, to the height of the ramps either side. A full width spoiler was then added. "It added only minute extra weight and cost only a touch more drag but provided a lot more downforce".

The result was impressive. Horsman again: "from Stavelot to La Source the back end really stuck, the driver could keep his foot down in top..."

Indeed, the driver only had to change down for La Source! That was with a 4.9 engine, JWA having now accepted this development. But a 4.9 litre 917 didn't secure fastest lap on Friday — that honour went to Ickx' Ferrari in 3′24.4″. The 917s were in trouble with tyres creeping inwards on the rim. Horsman explains that centrifugal force was sucking the tyre off the bead seat, letting air escape, causing hairy moments for Kinnunen, Siffert and Redman, who somehow managed to hold his car as it went sideways at around 160 m.p.h on an uphill bend. He arrived back at the pits "somewhat shaken, with the tyre flat". In retrospect, it was realized that the phenomenon had been responsible for a flat that Hailwood had suffered right at the end of the Le Mans test weekend.

That evening all the wheels were stripped down and Horsman and the lads went down the road to Liege where they sand blasted rims all night, slowly and patiently rotating each to roughen up its surface. With that the tyres stuck to the rims and, having put the new tail in place, Rodriguez went around in 3′19.8″ to claim an unfamiliar pole position. Siffert similarly outqualified local boy Ickx, while Elford was unhappy with his handling. In addition to a second Salzburg car there were also 917s from AAW and Gesipa, while Ferrari had three coupes (but not Amon) and there was one private 512. This time there were no works 3.0 litre cars...

Elford's problem was traced to a cracked frame, but he never overcame the handicap of a midfield start. This race saw Rodriguez and Siffert go out front (once rubbing bodywork at Eau Rouge) with Ickx shadowing. Siffert had a slow first stop due to a fuel rig malfunction, then Rodriguez lost 1¾ minutes in the pits due to a chunking tyre. That left the Ickx/Surtees car ahead, with the 917s catching as it started to suffer oil pressure fluctuations. Redman overtook Surtees on lap 35, Rodriguez on lap 37, the Mexican having cut a remarkable 3′16.5″ reducing his handicap. However, he was out of synch on fuel stops and Kinnunen started his sole, mid race stint behind Surtees. The Finn kept pace with the Ferrari, only to stop at Stavelot. The gearbox input shaft had failed.

Siffert/Redman refuelled from the sister car's rig and managed to get almost a lap ahead of the troubled Ferrari, while Elford/Ahrens claimed third, Herrmann/Attwood sixth close behind the

The early stag the Spa 1000 saw Siffert (n and Rodrigue vying for supremacy on of the world's fastest road r circuits. Rodr retired but to honour of fas lap; Siffert w (Gulf archive)

JWA had a
lified tail for
magnificent
weeping Spa
circuit with
swept valley
loor and full
th spoiler. It
glue the car
e high speed
turns.

AAW car and three laps down. The AAW machine had crashed.

After Spa came the Nurburgring, where the 908/3 was again in its element. It wasn't significantly faster, but it was more fuel efficient and less tiring to drive. For the record, Siffert cut a 7′47.7″ test lap in a 917K. The Gesipa car started but retired with a damaged wheel. Elford/Ahrens led home a one-two for Salzburg entered 908/3s after Siffert/Redman seized and Kinnunen lightly shunted the other JWA car. He had reportedly been unhappy about racing following the death of a close friend in a practice accident.

The week after the 'Ring 1000 kms. Rodriguez won the Belgian Grand Prix for BRM without challenging his 917 lap record due to the installation of chicanes to satisfy the Grand Prix driver safety lobby. The Francorchamps 1000 km. stood as the fastest ever road race.

Thanks to the 'Ring triumph Porsche had secured another world title, but next came the challenge that counted most. Wyer refused the latest Le Mans *Langheck*, preferring the proven 917K: it was left to the back-up team to counter Ferrari's *Coda Lunga* with similar technology. In fact, one long tail car was given to Salzburg, one to the Martini team that had been running private 908/2s through the season. That left JWA with three 917Ks, Salzburg with two. The third JWA car (Hobbs/Hailwood) and the Salzburg 917Ks (Herrmann/Attwood and Steinemann/Spoerry) had 4.5 litre engines, as did the other 917 in the race. This was from the AAW team and, taking over Piper's entry, was driven by Piper/van Lennep. It was backed by Steve McQueen's film company Solar Productions, present to make an epic out of the epic. However, like all others of the five JWA-support cars, it was prepared by the factory. Piëch couldn't afford to lose this one...

The opposition included no less than 11 examples of the Ferrari 512S, spearheaded by four works cars and two Filipinetti cars running long tails, all six running factory prepared engines. Like arch-rival Piech, Forghieri believed in numbers...

Matra and Alfa Romeo made what could only be token efforts. This was truly a battle of giants.

The Slough prepared cars had JWA's usual 24 hour accessories: back-up alternators and batteries, a larger starter motor, quick change headlights, and so forth. New was less front wheel offset (longer wishbones maintaining the same track) with the aim of improving directional stability and reducing steering kick-back. There was also a modified gearbox with redesigned shafts, the Spa failure having been traced to a fatigue crack from a radial oil passage.

The most obvious novelty was another JWA tail

modification. Following advice from John Wimpenny, the Chief Research Engineer at Hawker-Siddeley, the team had removed the upswept valley infill and full width spoiler and had substituted an aerofoil to NACA section 4412. Fabricated from aluminium by JWA, this was less sensitive to the degree of yaw and was manually adjustable. It allowed the ramp spoilers to be run at a lower angle and offered higher downforce with no more drag than the standard tail (and MIRA test results suggested a drag reduction of 3% if the level of rear downforce was maintained). Horsman says, "it put more downforce onto the rear wheels. It shifted the centre of pressure rearwards slightly but that did not present a problem of instability in crosswinds".

Scrutineering revealed that, if Ferrari now had the power to match Porsche, it still carried the best part of 50 kg. weight penalty. However, Vaccarella was very fast in qualifying, taking his works *Coda Lunga* around in 3′20.0″, only 0.2 seconds slower than Elford in the Salzburg streamliner. Siffert was one second slower in the fastest 917K, third fastest overall. The 917K for Steinemann/Spoerry, very much a reserve car, was withdrawn after Spoerry had a practice accident in a 908/2, then failed a medical check-up.

The race saw Elford and Siffert the early pace makers. Vaccarella lasted only half an hour, a con rod failing. Then rain set in. The 917K was easier to drive in the wet and Redman started pulling away from Ahrens. Meanwhile, it was Kinnunen's turn to suffer a broken con rod. Horsman: "it was an inclusion in the forging. It should have been X-rayed before it had been accepted into the factory". He reckons that running so many cars saw corners cut...

"Pedro should have won the race, he had the right car and the right attitude, everything. He was let down by a broken con rod — the last thing you expect to break from Porsche".

As the rain continued to fall there was drama for Ferrari, a pile up costing two of the three remaining works cars plus both Filipinetti runners. Meanwhile, Redman continued running away from Ahrens until a lost wheel balance weight reversed the order. Soon after the three-hour mark Hailwood crashed in heavy rain at the Dunlop Bridge. Then Redman retook the lead in the team's sole surviving car.

Six hours: Siffert/Redman plus three laps, Elford/Ahrens — Ickx/Schetty. The three other 917s leading the pursuit. In the eighth hour the Salzburg streamliner fell back, hampered by a deflating tyre. In the tenth hour Ickx hit a puddle and crashed at the chicane. And in the eleventh hour Siffert missed a gear...

Herrmann/Attwood led into the second half of the race, chased by the two *Langhecks*. Neither came through to upset its run to victory. Sure enough, of Piëch's six main hopes, two retired through driver error, two through mechanical failure. And while both the 917K and the 917LH around at the finish had suffered misfiring at various stages in the rain, Ferrari had fared worse...

Le Mans 1970 introduced a r Langheck *but became the ra* the Kurz. *The winning exam (above) was th the Salzburg t — the similar of Siffert (righ and Rodriguez both failed to the night. Por was delighted win at last bu JWA felt its chances of vic had been compromised the marque's support for th Salzburg team*

Of the second string entries, the AAW car had retired following a blow out on the Mulsanne but two private Ferraris had made the finish, collecting fourth and fifth places.

The Thursday after the race Stuttgart's Lord Mayor Dr. Arnulf Klett received Dr. Ferry Porsche and his first and second placed drivers at the Town Hall to thank them in the name of the city, the cars having been driven up from Zuffenhausen through its streets, led by police escort.

Hans Herrmann hung up his helmet on this happy note and for the Watkins Glen Six Hours in mid July the Salzburg cars were handled by Elford/Hulme and Ahrens/Attwood. Again they ran in Porsche Audi USA colours. The JWA cars retained their rear wings, now with endplates, and sported small horizontal fins over the rear wheel opening. They were equipped with cast iron discs that had been cross-drilled in between their curved cooling vanes saving over 1.5 kg. per wheel. These so called 'Gruyere' discs had first been tried at the

November '69 Daytona test. Run with calipers having two pairs of 42 mm. pistons, they increased wear by around 5% but ran significantly cooler and overcame taper wear, keeping the linings cleaner as the material rubbed off was taken away by the holes. There were also modified rims with a small ridge to retain the tyre bead: sand blasting was no longer necessary.

The engines had modified crankcase breathers with outlets front and rear and for the first time a rev limiter was available. Nevertheless, a missed shift would send revs soaring before the limiter could respond.

In addition to the four regular 917s, the AAW car was entered by the Martini team. Ferrari only had two spyders, but Andretti was back in the team and again overshadowed the Porsches in practice. He led from the rolling start but Siffert got ahead in traffic. Rodriguez ,meanwhile, lost ground by inadvertently switching off a fuel pump while reaching to flash the headlights. He then got his act together and proceeded to overhaul both Andretti (suffering overheating fuel pumps) and Siffert. Within the first hour it started raining and Siffert's engine started misfiring at high r.p.m. He assumed it was water in the electrics but in fact the rev limiter had retarded itself and he lost almost a lap to Rodriguez. At the first fuel stop both cars had their rev limiters disconnected.

During the second hour Rodriguez came up to

Martini chases JWA at the Osterreichring. O this occasion, neither Porsche team had the measure of Ferra Had the rival 51 lasted the race, t scene of the 917' first victory and subsequent transformation might well have been the scene o its most significa defeat.

lap Siffert: in the words of Wyer's autobiography, "the rivalry which had been latent throughout the season really came into the open..." A certain amount of pushing and shoving ended with crumpled righthand side bodywork for Rodriguez and a punctured left front tyre for Siffert. Redman rejoined over a lap behind but proved able to make up a lot of ground on Kinnunen. Rodriguez then lost time having the door repaired but came through to win by a comfortable margin after both cars had been slightly delayed having the rear crankcase breather closed off as the catch tanks had been over-filling...

With the collision and the breather problems, it was fortunate that both 512s had fuel system problems. Andretti had to be satisfied with third after losing a couple of laps due to the fuel system malady, while Elford's only reward was a distant fourth following severe tyre chunking that cost many stops. The second Salzburg car ran out of fuel on the final lap but finished sixth while the Martini entry was ninth after a broken shock absorber had cost much ground.

The following day was a Can Am race in which all three JWA cars were run, Redman driving the spare. Rodriguez lost his engine, Redman suffered a puncture and fell to seventh, but Siffert finished second on the same lap as the only surviving works McLaren after a splendid run. Attwood and Elford finished, respectively, third and fourth for Salzburg, while van Lennep was sixth for Martini.

July and August saw two factory cars (004 and 013) loaned to Solar Productions and in action at Le Mans for the benefit of the cameras. Piper crashed heavily in 013 at White House, finishing up 50 yards off the circuit with his leg broken in three places. The car was rebuilt around frame no. 034.

Imola in mid September saw Rodriguez and Redman take on the works Ferrari of Merzario/Giunti in a 500 km. non-championship race. Rodriguez damaged 016 against the barrier avoiding a backmarker and Redman won in 026. He subsequently announced his impending retirement, with only the Osterreichring race in mid October to conclude the season.

For the Osterreichring Ferrari had a heavily revised car, the 512M. Most significant of many improvements were new (spyder-inspired) aerodynamics and less weight (812 kg.), while Ferrari was now using chrome liners and could get an honest 616 b.h.p. One example was entered, for Ickx who, in spite of fuel feed bothers, was only fractionally off Rodriguez' pole time. And the race revealed the true potential of the car: Ickx ran away, reaching the pole time within a few laps on full tanks. The 917 had met its match. Horsman acknowledges that Ferrari was superior in Austria. "The 917 had been so much better in 1970 than before that everyone had been revelling in its new found performance. But the competition had hotted up at Zeltweg and a handling deficiency showed up. We were starting to fall behind".

The Ferrari demonstration lasted the best part of two hours, then the alternator failed. Porsche could breath a sigh of relief. The race was now down to JWA versus Salzburg cars in the hands of Elford/Attwood and Ahrens/Marko, while the works Alfa Romeo team gave chase. JWA had only one car running, Rodriguez having retired early with a broken tappet. With Siffert unhappy with his handling and with Elford's car having lost three laps replacing the oil cooler, Ahrens/Marko were looking strong.

Salzburg's hopes evaporated with its fuel: the car ran out due to a miscalculation. JWA was set for a comfortable cruise to victory when, with 13 laps to go, a tappet broke. Siffert limped home on 11 cylinders: had the tappet broken sooner it would have made a gift of the race to Alfa Romeo. Elford/Ahrens finished fourth, after further delays.

Ingegnere *Giac Caliri waves t new Ferrari 51 out onto the sweeping Osterreichring circuit. A hea modified deriv of the 512S (homologated evolution of t basic model), aerodynamica improved run with 616 b.h.p engine was fa than the 4.9 l engined 917.*

More for less

Of the thirteen and a half kilometers constituting a lap of Le Mans, three and a half were driven as one long flat out blind. Through careful attention to aerodynamics it was possible to gain valuable seconds here though, as Wyer points out in his autobiography, it was as easy to lose them again around the rest of the circuit if low drag achievement necessitated a significant handling forfeit, as had traditionally been the case. And an easier handling car would be less tiring to drive. However, even for low and high drag configurations offering equal lap times the low drag car would have two major advantages: it would be better able to overtake on the best place, the straight (and therefore would not necessarily be more tiring to *race*) and it would consume less fuel, wasting less time in the pits (particularly significant over 24 hours).

As we have seen, fuel consumption was perceived as a key factor in the struggle to keep the air cooled engine competitive. "*Langheck* development was always for fuel consumption", Piëch confirms. And so it was that a major effort went into the production of a more stable low drag car for 1970. The aim was to maintain the original machine's drag co-efficient of 0.30 with greater stability and it was, of course, clear that further development of movable aerodynamic devices wouldn't be tolerated. A lot of wind tunnel work went into a revised body shape which in February '70 was submitted for homologation as an evolution of the original, retaining windscreen, roof, doors and rear canopy shape.

As revealed in March 1970, the new shape incorporated a higher-downforce nose, an extended version of the regular 1970 *Kurz* nose. In fact, the original higher downforce nose revealed at the Osterreichring test in October of '69 had been taken out of the *Langheck* development programme. More front end downforce was seen as essential with the loss of movable flaps and consequent danger of flying. The version now offered for the *Langheck* featured full headlight fairings reaching right to the front, split (yet 1970 *Kurz*-style) inlets for radiator and brake cooling and an original-style divided radiator air outlet to vent air around the sides of the windscreen. It also had small vents to the rear of each wheel arch to help reduce wheel well pressure and temperature.

Behind the unchanged midriff (retaining the pronounced dip in the body line either side of the cockpit superstructure) was a refashioned version of the original tail, retaining a similar length and similar general form, with upswept aerodynamic underside behind the rear wheels. While the rear window's shape was unchanged it was left unvented and two transverse slots behind provided breathing for the engine bay. The first and larger of these, positioned between the rear wheels, had rounded corners and an upward-reaching circumferential lip which kissed a low pressure area. It drew in air for the engine while behind was a small rectangular slot for transmission cooling.

Although the general form of the tail was familiar it featured larger stabilizing fins, reaching back from the latter part of each rear wheel bulge to the very end of the deck. Between them the deck, having sloped gently down from the rear wheel axis, had an upswept end.

Overall,and in contrast to 1969, there was little similarity between the shape of *Kurz* and *Langheck* versions of the 1970 917. Of course, mechanically the *Langheck* incorporated the various modifications seen on the sister model. Running 15" rear rims increased the frontal area by 12% over 1969 but the revised shape was claimed to retain a drag co-efficient of 0.30.

The revised …gheck *shape* …ed at the Le …ans trials in … featured an …ented engine canopy with …y shaped air behind it to …he flat 12 to breathe.*

Easy for Vic

The new *Langheck* body was produced in March and was tested at Volkswagen's Wolfsburg proving ground in April, prior to the Le Mans test weekend. Ahrens went out in the first car (040), running dry tyres. Alas, it started to rain lightly. Now, the Wolfsburg high speed test track (with an 8 km. straight) ran through the woods and with the rain came gusts of wind down clearings in the wood and across the track. The light rain wouldn't have been a problem without those gusts. The combination of reduced friction and a perpendicular side force catching the fins (which provide stability in the face of lateral forces, which are normally from an acute angle) proved too much for the slippery-shaped car. On only his second lap, not yet going for a time, Ahrens was caught out.

Flegl: "having big fins, the wind upset the car more. With the wind and the fins the forces got so high that there wasn't enough friction on the damp track... the fins would normally have stabilized the car but the forces got too high and it just broke loose".

By all accounts Ahrens was a lucky guy, escaping with bruised ribs which forced him to miss Brands Hatch a few days later. The car was scrap. That following weekend a brand new, rapidly assembled *Langheck* (041) was run at Le Mans, driven mainly by Linge. As we have noted, the test weekend was also wet. The car was fitted with a lift measuring rod connected to the suspension and protruding through the left front wing within the driver's line of sight but it wasn't taken over 190 m.p.h.

Wyer says in his autobiography that the car "was a pig to drive, and all the drivers hated it". Subsequently it was also written off at Wolfsburg, and JWA decided only to run *Kurz* models in the 24 hour race. The second accident befell Kauhsen, again in the wet. He had rain tyres fitted, but went aquaplaning. Flegl: "Kauhsen didn't see some standing water until it was too late. He spun and hit a post. The car was badly damaged but Kauhsen wasn't hurt at all".

041 had only run 230 kms, 040 less than 30. The two cars presented at Le Mans were new, and featured a revised shape. Between the test weekend and the race some two months later further wind tunnel work had been done in conjunction with the Paris based SERA design office run by Charles Deutsch, well known for a succession of low drag Le Mans cars. Important developments were a concave shaping for the nose

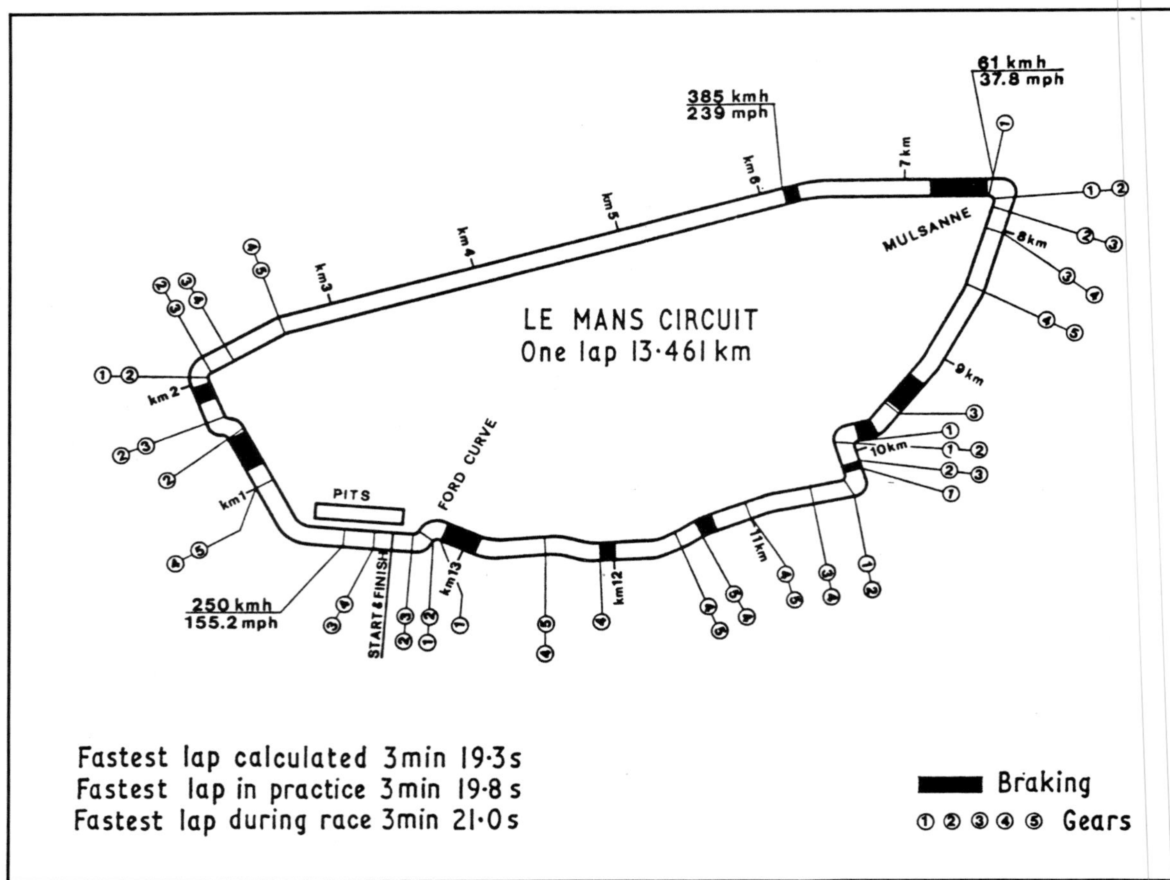

The Langheck *shape run in 1970 24 Hour was modified that seen at t weekend, wit exposed engi cooling scoop projecting fr rear deck an concave fron rear deck sur*

Having been data on all a of Porsche r performance the mid Sixti 1970 the Por computer wa to make accu predictions a the performa new models, the relevant o on engine ou drag co-effici and suchlike. is how it anticipated th Langheck *in at Le Mans 1*

surface and a remodelling of the rear deck. The latter had the window removed to expose the engine as on the *Kurz* model while transverse slots were shunned by the more obviously concave surface behind. This improved stability at the cost of a slight drag penalty. In addition an aerofoil was slung between the tail fins. This was adjustable, providing an easy method of varying rear downforce. Detail changes saw the lower edge of the oil cooler intake cut back to the cooler, larger brake cooling inlets either side, NACA ducts for cockpit ventilation and scoops rather than a slot for transmission cooling.

The uniquely-five-speed-equipped, polyurethane-sandwich-bodied Le Mans race cars (042 and 043) carried a 25 kg. weight penalty biased towards the rear but were reckoned to have a drag coefficient of 0.36 and to have a top speed advantage of just over 20 k.p.h. Of course, the new shape car wasn't a proven proposition, while in qualifying Elford took pole only 1.3 seconds ahead of the fastest JWA 917K (with similar 4.9 engine). His time was 0.5 seconds slower than had been predicted by the Porsche computer on the basis of a 239 m.p.h. top speed. The genuine speed attained was somewhere in the region of 225 - 235 m.p.h. The second, Martini-entered car conducted by Kauhsen and Larrousse (who regularly drove a Martini team 908/2) ran a 4.5 engine and qualified 12th fastest. It caused a certain amount of shock by turning out in a light green and violet psychedelic colour scheme produced by Anatole Lapine's styling department which was not appreciated by all within the house of Porsche.

Ferrari ran long tails on all its top entries (the four works cars plus the two Filipinetti cars), essentially an extended version of the standard tail, with choice of high or low downforce nose as available for the regular 512S. The *Coda Lunga* was somewhat heavier than the Porsche *Langheck* yet with 595 b.h.p. chrome engine Vaccarella qualified only 0.3 seconds slower than Elford. The Ferrari tail was reckoned to be worth 15 k.p.h. but all the works crews other than Ickx/Schetty opted for the higher downforce nose, which required more rear spoiler to balance, improving overall driveability.

Elford was enthusiastic about 917 042: "it was chalk and cheese compared to the '69 car — I was very happy to drive it. The car still had to be *committed* to a corner but it was more driveable, and was flat through the kink... It was still quite hard work, predictably understeering again — you don't want to lose the rear at high speed — but this year you could place it accurately and it didn't zig-zag if the back started to come out. It was superb through the Esses — as if on rails. The short tail car braked better and was more manoeuvrable in traffic but at Le Mans you go past people on pure speed — that's my philosophy — so the long tail car worked better.

"At the start of the race Siffert and I cleared off. Each lap I gained 400 or 500 yards on the Mulsanne which he caught back, a little bit under braking, a little bit speed through the corners but he couldn't pass. I could keep him behind until the Mulsanne again. It was a lot easier work for me..."

In the dry Elford managed a 3′21.0″ lap which would stand as the record, while even in the wet the *Langheck* was flat through the kink, if less comfortable than the 917K. However, on Saturday night Elford/Ahrens were delayed by slow punctures and a lighting problem which left them fifth at midnight. Nevertheless, Elford was confident of regaining ground: "I was quick at night in the rain thanks to my rally background. At one stage I was making up a lap an hour on the leading cars".

Elford did a long stint and by dawn the car was up to second, ahead of the sister *Langheck* (which was misfiring) and closing on the Salzburg 917K. Then Ahrens had a bump with a 911 which called for a certain amount of tape on the body and finally a valve spring fractured at 8.30 am. Of course, the Martini *Langheck* went on to collect second, even though it was badly affected by its rain-induced misfire. It is significant that while the winning car had consumed 45.2 litres for every 100 km., the *Langheck* survivor had only required 38.6. It won the Index of Consumption.

The Porsche Salzburg ent Langheck dr Vic Elford a Kurt Ahrens the swiftest c seven-strong fleet at Le M 1970. Howe was only marginally fa than the JW 917Ks and li JWA cars fa last the night

ZUFFENHAUSEN BRIEFING

The Chameleon

Having been rechristened as *Group 5* for 1970, the homologated sports car class had been given only two years to live. Porsche would consequently have to develop a new 3.0 litre engine for 1972 World Championship races and to keep up in the power stakes it would need water cooled four valve heads. A design had been put in hand. At the same time there was an attractive alternative in the Can Am series which, as we have seen, Porsche Audi USA was keen to exploit. If the 5.0 litre 917 could overshadow the 5.0 litre Chevrolet, could not a 7.0 litre 917 overshadow the 7.0 litre Chevrolet?

The 917 engine could only be enlarged to 5.4 litres but thanks to its central drive four extra cylinders could be added (two either end), producing a hefty 7.2 litre displacement. Such a derivative had been put in hand. It hadn't been ready for the 1970 series but Porsche Audi USA was hoping to run a trial programme this year. And Zuffenhausen was now enthusiastic about Can Am, thanks partly to the imposition of a 650 kg. minimum weight limit on 3.0 litre prototypes: running a lighter car than the opposition was to have been a key factor in any 1972 World Championship campaign. Can Am, of course, did not impose a minimum weight, and it did not offer any four valve race engine opposition.

Although no new Porsche Can Am car had been fielded in 1970 the marque's colours had, of course, been flown by JWA and Salzburg at Watkins Glen (with Siffert taking that excellent second place) and two months later privateer Tony Dean had taken a somewhat fortuitous win at Road Atlanta in a 908/2. In Europe, a new German-based six-race Group 7 'Interseries' championship had rekindled interest in American-style Big Banger racing. The fledgeling series had been won by Neuhaus in the Gusipa Rivets 917 coupe. By the end of 1970 a Can Am future was a certainty for Porsche and the possibility of exploiting exhaust gas turbocharging — almost unknown in the field of road racing — was under investigation.

JWA had recently approached Porsche (quite independently of Porsche Audi USA) with a view to running an exploratory Can Am programme during the latter half of 1971 and this possibility was still under discussion. In the meantime there was another Group 5 season to contest, one for which homologation provisions were relaxed. In the light of the speed of the 512M certain rumour-mongers anticipated a 16 cylinder 917 coupe but this had never been on the cards. Nevertheless, the Porsche Press Office did produce a spoof press release offering data on a "5000cc 16 cylinder engine" based on the concept of two of the old 2.2 litre 8 cylinder Type 771 engines either side of a 917 type central drive. As the release went out before April 1 the story was printed unquestioningly by its targets, confusing historians for years to come! In fact, as we shall see, Porsche did have some interesting developments up its sleeve to counter a stronger Ferrari attack, but that attack had been called off. Ferrari had decided that its response to the coming regulation change would be on-track development of a 3.0 litre prototype via participation in Group 6 this season.

On the face of it JWA would have no opposition from a works Group 5 team in 1971. However, the team was concerned over the amount of works support that the back up team had been getting, reckoning that it should have been able to fight Ferrari without the additional pressure of racing another factory supported operation. JWA was racing for the glory of Porsche *and* Gulf and had often found Salzburg its major opponent. As we have seen, when it had felt uneasy about an unproven development (such as the 4.9 litre engine) it had learnt that it was a question of race it, or race against it.

Horsman echoes the concern expressed in Wyer's autobiography, observing that: "Piëch often wanted to try something new — the engineer's approach ...Luckily, Porsche had us winning races for them..." The Salzburg team had now been disbanded but the Martini team had taken over its resources, to become the official back up. Horsman reckons Porsche's agreements with its back up teams were sometimes in conflict with the JWA contract ("so we had to be a bit cleverer...")

On the other hand, technical co-operation between JWA and Porsche had always been good and, for example, Piëch had helped JWA investigate the possibility of building its own engines in the interest of cutting down the supply lines. Late in 1970 the team had built one engine on a trial basis, running it on the Vandervell dyno, although as the dyno had inadequate air flow for the cooling system it couldn't run full load. Horsman recalls: "It took a colossal amount of man-hours to build the first engine. Porsche had its act well together on engine building. If it had been a real advantage we would have done it but it wasn't worth it".

The JWA driver line up continued to feature Siffert and Rodriguez (both now works BRM Grand Prix teamsters), but now all its drivers were

Right, in co
new colo
JWA's p
This year E
rapid 'ba
entry wore
livery.
Buenos A
succe
passing Ro
only to r
fuel feed b

38
MARTINI

under contract to Gulf. Redman had retired to South Africa while Kinnunen's contract hadn't been renewed so there were two new faces, those of Bell and Oliver. Bell was a Formula Two star with some good 512S drives to his credit while Oliver was, of course, a former Le Mans winner and he additionally had Formula One experience.

The Martini team was joined by Elford and Ahrens and would continue to employ two works-blessed drivers from its 1970 908 squad: Larrousse and Marko (with Lins and Porsche Cup winner van Lennep in reserve). Run by former driver Hans-Dieter Dechent, it was to enjoy vastly increased financial support from the Martini International Club via Martini Germany. The team was based in Saarbrucken but its mechanics travelled to Stuttgart to prepare its three ex-Salzburg cars. In 1970 its 908/2s had been supported by a factory engineer. This year factory assistance would extend to the loan of 908/3s for the Targa Florio and Nurburgring, and of a Le Mans *Langheck* once more. As with the Salzburg team, its engines were prepared by the Customer Service Department and ran on Shell.

In fact, the Martini team had already warmed up for the coming season by sending a car to the Kyalami 9 hours in November. Driven by Siffert and Ahrens, it had been soundly thrashed by a works 512M. Although Ferrari had now set that project aside, it had ensured that its prime customers had M-spec conversion kits...

If you believe accompanying Porsche Press Release you believe that illustrates an alternative 5. engine for 19 having 16 cylinders—th would have b some Ferrari baiter!

In the pipeline

To meet any challenge, Porsche had developments underway that would extract more power and save weight. None of these, however, would be seen until the season got well into its stride: thanks to Ferrari's switch to Group 6 the pressure was off.

A full five litre engine was on the drawing board and under investigation were Nikasil liners and beryllium pistons. Nikasil was a nickel-silicon carbide coating developed by Mahle primarily for the NSU Wankel engine. For years Mahle chrome liners had been run by Porsche but chrome was a problem when used in conjunction with aluminium: it was not unknown in race engines for chrome plating to lift, destroying a piston, Piëch explains. Nikasil was reckoned to work better with aluminium, and to offer better friction characteristics.

Beryllium (of which the dust is poisonous) had

paration of a ' at Slough in cember 1970, for the early art to JWA's cond Porsche season.

af, in colour *peat a success driguez d a gritty e rebuild of rbox by the ads. Pictured g the sight dly crippled ored to re (left to lan Hearn, nes, o Cuoghi Ramirez. In re photo, ez is seen ng with Yorke (left) n Horsman practice. In top e early in , Siffert is Bell a car to retire t.*

76
1

Y LANE
Gulf
2

Gulf
2

LAPS
688 2
DA

LAPS
DA

already been employed in the form of extremely light brake discs with chrome-plated faces. Porsche had bought five such discs for its mid Sixties hillclimb car from America. Piëch says that the prototype beryllium piston came from Britain and was one third lighter than the aluminium item it was to replace. It was also more heat resistant, allowing a slightly higher compression ratio to be run. As with the discs, a major drawback was cost: DM 3,000 per piston, or the price of a family car to equip each engine! Beryllium was also being investigated for the flywheel, but it wasn't clear how an adequate starter ring could be incorporated.

Although the beryllium discs hadn't been raced on the 917, Porsche's own copper-beryllium alternative was under development, offering a better heat flow. It promised higher efficiency as well as lower unsprung weight. Another important area of weight saving under consideration was a magnesium chassis frame. This promised to be stiffer yet lighter but was even more difficult to weld.

The 917 frame was notoriously whippy: with both ends jacked up the doors couldn't be closed. And sometimes Cuoghi had found it impossible to fit the engine bay bracing struts after installing an engine without jacking up one side of the car! However, he confirms that on the track, "the 917 frame was working well even if it was flexing. It was flexing like hell and going like hell, so I really don't know..."

Aerodynamically, the only significant *Kurz* development for 1971 was an alternative tail, suitable for faster circuits. However, Horsman recalls that lack of front end downforce was a potential weakness: "if we had been pushed by Ferrari in '71 we might have redesigned the front end".

The tail Porsche had in the Experimental Department was lower ahead of the rear wheels, had the valley behind the engine filled in and had a slightly concave deck flanked by fins. Porsche wind tunnel tests suggested a 15% drag reduction with 20% less rear downforce, 20% more on the front. It was to be used in conjunction with a slight remodelling of the flanks, immediately behind the front arches. Here the body bulged slightly to improve air flow from the wheel wells.

As they started the season, as early as January and as far away from home as Argentina, the 917Ks fielded by JWA and Martini were, not surprisingly, virtually identical to those seen at the Osterreichring in 1970. The only modifications were detail ones, such as a sightly revised gearbox. It had been discovered that the Martini *Langheck* had finished Le Mans with a broken third gear pinion — this was blamed on flexing of the shaft and there was an increased shaft diameter for 1971. The 1971 917K was certainly not a new car, but its price tag was unfamiliar, up from DM 140,000 to DM 280,000.

The JWA-fielded 917Ks were stripped to the nut and bolt (titanium, of course) at Slough between races.

A tarantola

Ferrari might have abandoned Group 5 but it had sold M-spec conversion kits to two very professional teams: Filipinetti and Roger Penske Racing. Penske, of course, had done a splendid job for Lola at Daytona in '69 and this year hoped to do the same for Ferrari at the three North American races and Le Mans. Filipinetti would contest the European season. Penske added some modifications of its own, including aerodynamically superior slab (rather than inward curving) sides, a full width rear wing and an Indy-style dry break refuelling system to speed pit stops.

The works Ferrari was a pretty little spyder based on Formula One technology, with the latest 180 degree V12 engine in the back. The new engine had shown Cosworth-beating power in late '70 Formula One races. It was state of the art with four valves per cylinder, narrow valve angle and flat topped piston, and ran chrome cylinders. It was all-alloy, and relied heavily on oil, and to a lesser extent (unforced) air, for cooling its crankcase and the lower (inner) portion of each of its two banks of six cylinders. It had a steel crank running in only four main bearings and titanium con rods and was gear driven off the clutch end. It ran Marelli 'Dinoplex' transistorised ignition, Lucas injection and on an 11.5:1 compression ratio was rated as producing 450 b.h.p. at 10,800 r.p.m. in endurance trim.

The 312P, as the new Group 6 challenger was known, featured the usual plated spaceframe chassis construction and ran on a 2220 mm. wheelbase. It was in every sense a 312B Formula One car with enclosed wheels, developed specifically for 1000 km. rather than 24 hour races. Weighing in at 585 kgs., it was very light and agile and promised to embarrass the Group 5 cars through tighter turns. With a power to weight ratio as good as a Group 5 coupe and a smaller frontal area it could be expected to make more of a mark than Alfa Romeo or Matra had done in 1970. Both Group 6 regulars would continue, with refined versions of their existing cars.

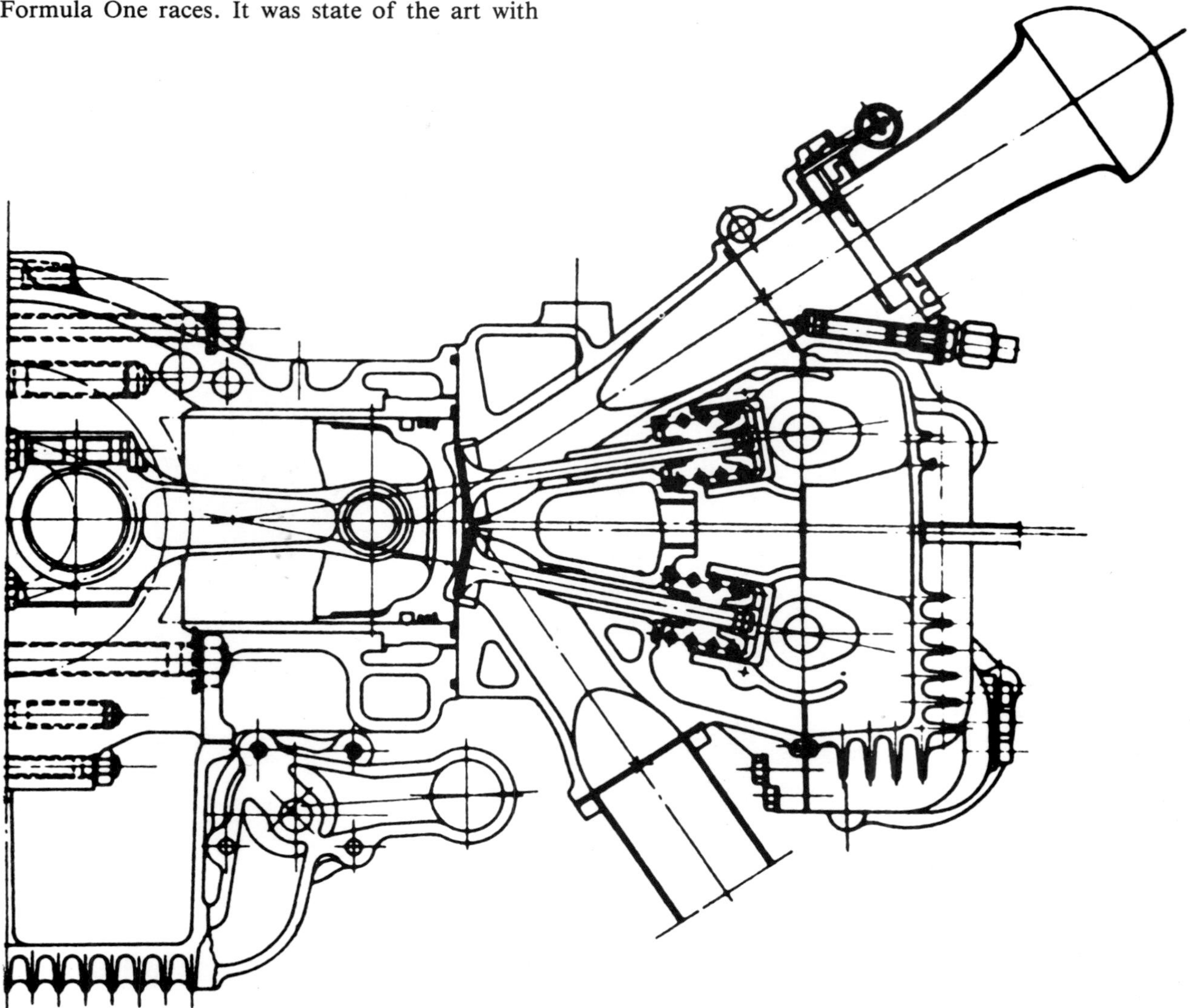

i's 180 degree engine was of litre capacity and had water cooled upper ıder and head ile relying on air, and more ıportantly, oil oling over the ntral portion.

af, in colour ytona traffic eaded by the cars of guez (no. 2) iffert. Taken opening lap, ıot shows Ferrari 512 ngers but not stest of the the Penske is out front.

1
Gulf
Gulf
2

GOOD YEAR
2
50

Repeat performance

The sight of a Group 6 car playing David to Porsche's Goliath was something quite novel. Buenos Aires was not the sort of circuit that that would have given 1970 lightweights any chance against the 5.0 litre heavyweights but here, early in January, was Ferrari's new 3.0 litre runner showing how it should be done. Of course, the car's power and weight did for Group 6 what the Porsche 917 had done for Group 4 (at far less expense). Giunti at the controls, the 312P failed to take pole position from the Rodriguez 917 by a scant four hundreths of a second.

The Rodriguez car had been all but eliminated by Oliver three days before, his new partner going off in unofficial practice. Jo Ramirez, new to the team, recalls, "it was a big mess! We had to cut away much of the front end and replace it. Everyone was surprised it could be repaired". As it was, a new windscreen and various suspension parts had to be flown in from the UK. Both JWA cars were in familiar trim, as were the Martini machines handled by Elford/Larrousse and Marko/van Lennep. There were also three customer cars, those of Ortiz Patino (a Bolivian millionaire who financed Racing Team Zitro (read Ortiz backwards) for godson race driver Dominique Martin), Reinhold Joest (whose little-used ex-Le Mans film car was sponsored and run by Auto Usdau, a Mannheim-based used Mercedes dealership) and Alex Soler-Roig.

Aside from the works Ferrari, the opposition comprised four 512s (of which one was the Filipinetti 512M), a works Matra and two equally familiar works Alfa Romeo prototypes. The second Martini car became a starting money special following an engine failure in Saturday qualifying — Dechent's team had no spare. Predictably the race featured Rodriguez, Giunti, Siffert and Elford, who finished lap one in that order after the cheeky red car had lept ahead at the off. It took Siffert six laps to pass, then he had to stop to clean oil off his screen.

Up front the race featured a great battle between Rodriguez and Elford, the Englishman enjoying a slight tyre advantage on the gravel strewn circuit: "I drove right around the outside of Rodriguez on a long, long 180 degree corner taken almost flat!" Elford subsequently pulled away at a couple of seconds a lap, before a fuel pump played up. Soon afterwards the first round of pit stops started, then came tragedy, Giunti colliding with Beltoise' stationary Matra in full view of the pits. The enormous impact killed the Italian and left the pit lane shocked, and with little heart for racing. Rodriguez/Oliver were delayed by a puncture, Elford/ Larrousse were

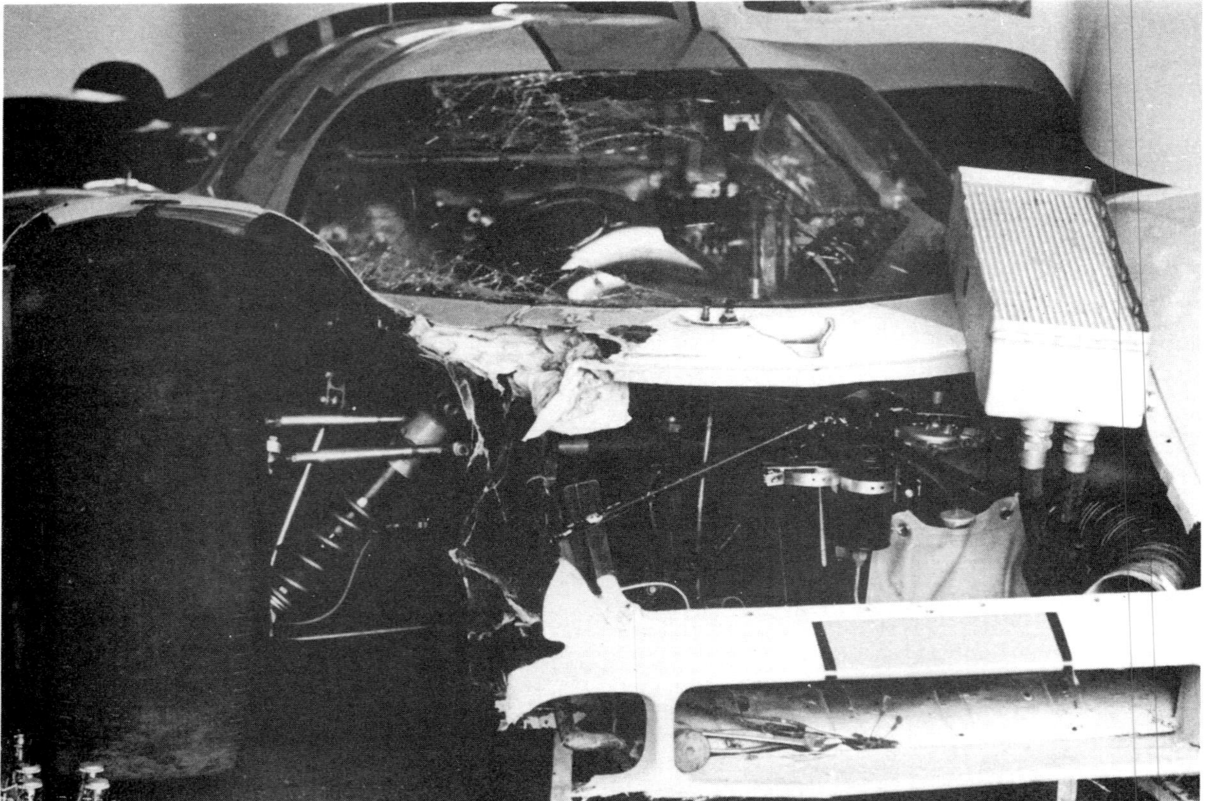

Rodriguez le… swift new 3.… at Buenos A… Maranello's … challenger se… standard for … prototypes, o… worrying to … runners.

Oliver starte… association w… Porsche 917 … shunting the … at Buenos Ai… unofficial tes… took a lot of … repair but st…

af, in colour
on from
and Brands
The
an 12 hour
w the
team car
/Larrousse
scoop the
s while in
Alfa
took a
six hour
e victorious
prototype,
is visible at
t behind the
orsches, the
312P (no.
its sister
55).
man with
elling
at Brands
s 917
driver
d Joest!

disqualified after the mechanics had changed the fuel pump out on the circuit, while Siffert/Bell ran troublefree to head a joyless one — two for JWA. Only one other 917 finished, the Zitro car, in tenth place.

From Argentina some of the cars were shipped direct to Florida for the Daytona 24 hour race at the end of the month, including the Martini 917s (crewed here by Elford/van Lennep and Marko/Lins), which arrived late and missed the first day of qualifying. Fresh 4.5 engines had been flown out from Europe. JWA had shipped out three fresh 4.9 litre cars (with roof windows once more) and had the new finned tail to try. Evaluated on the spare, it provided an extra 300 r.p.m. at the expense of stability. Horsman: "it was no great revelation, giving a slight decrease in both drag and downforce". The team stuck with the regular tail.

There was no works Group 6 opposition on this occasion, only half a dozen Ferrari 512 privateers to contend with. But one of those was the Roger Penske operation. Donohue took the Penske 512M round the circuit over a second quicker than anything else in first qualifying session which, under Daytona regulations, settled the top 10 grid positions.

The American-prepared Ferrari was equally impressive in the early stages of the race, Rodriguez having to use all his skill in traffic to get ahead. Then came the first round of pit stops: Penske turned its car around 7.5 seconds faster than JWA thanks to its Indy-style pressurized, dry break refuelling system. However, at its second stop the 512M needed new rear tyres, then came a series of setbacks which left Rodriguez and Siffert fighting Elford. The Siffert/Bell car was the first of these to go: Siffert had just retired to the motorhome when Bell strolled in. Bell recalls that, not yet having had a chance to relax, Siffert casually offered him a Coke before it clicked... The answer was that a con rod had let go while he was accelerating up the pit lane.

Not long afterwards Elford had cause to put into practice a recent lesson in the art of NASCAR racing: "as a Rookie, they tell you that if anything goes wrong on the banking you should turn the wheel to the left and put your foot on the brakes... I could see the wall going past every couple of seconds in the headlights, seemingly in slow

DUNLOP
51

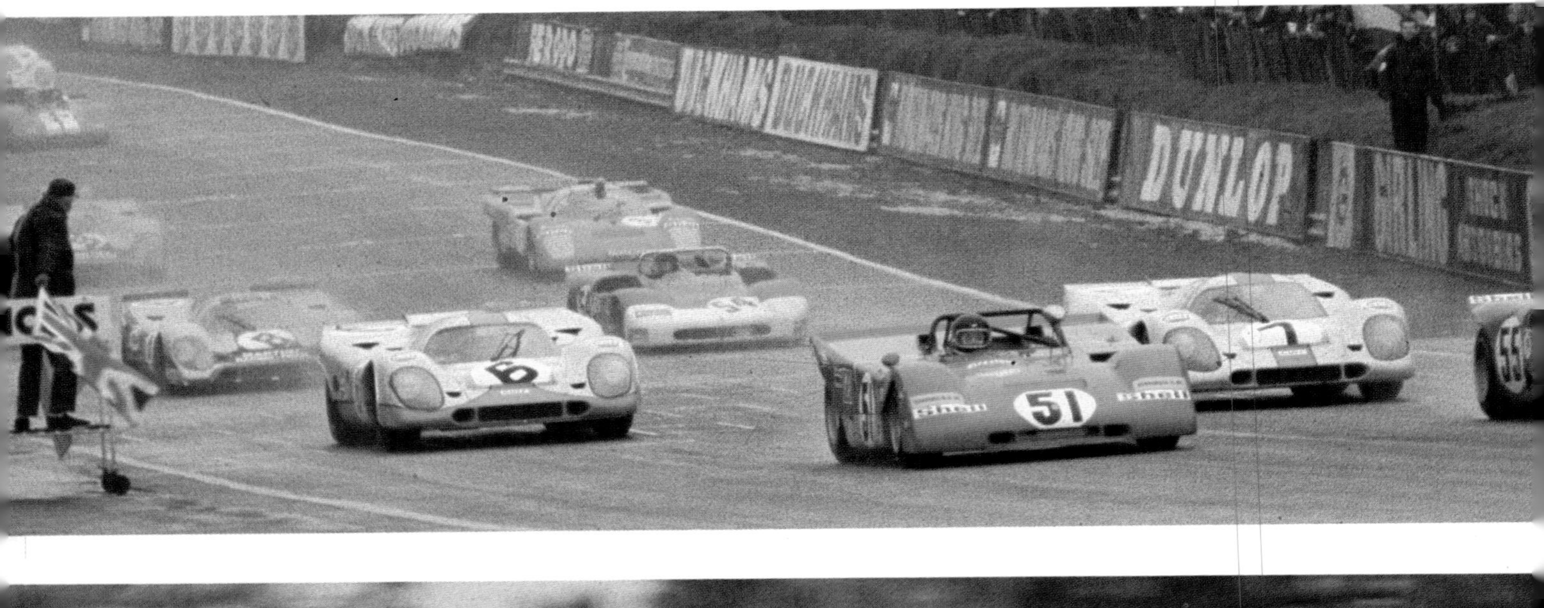

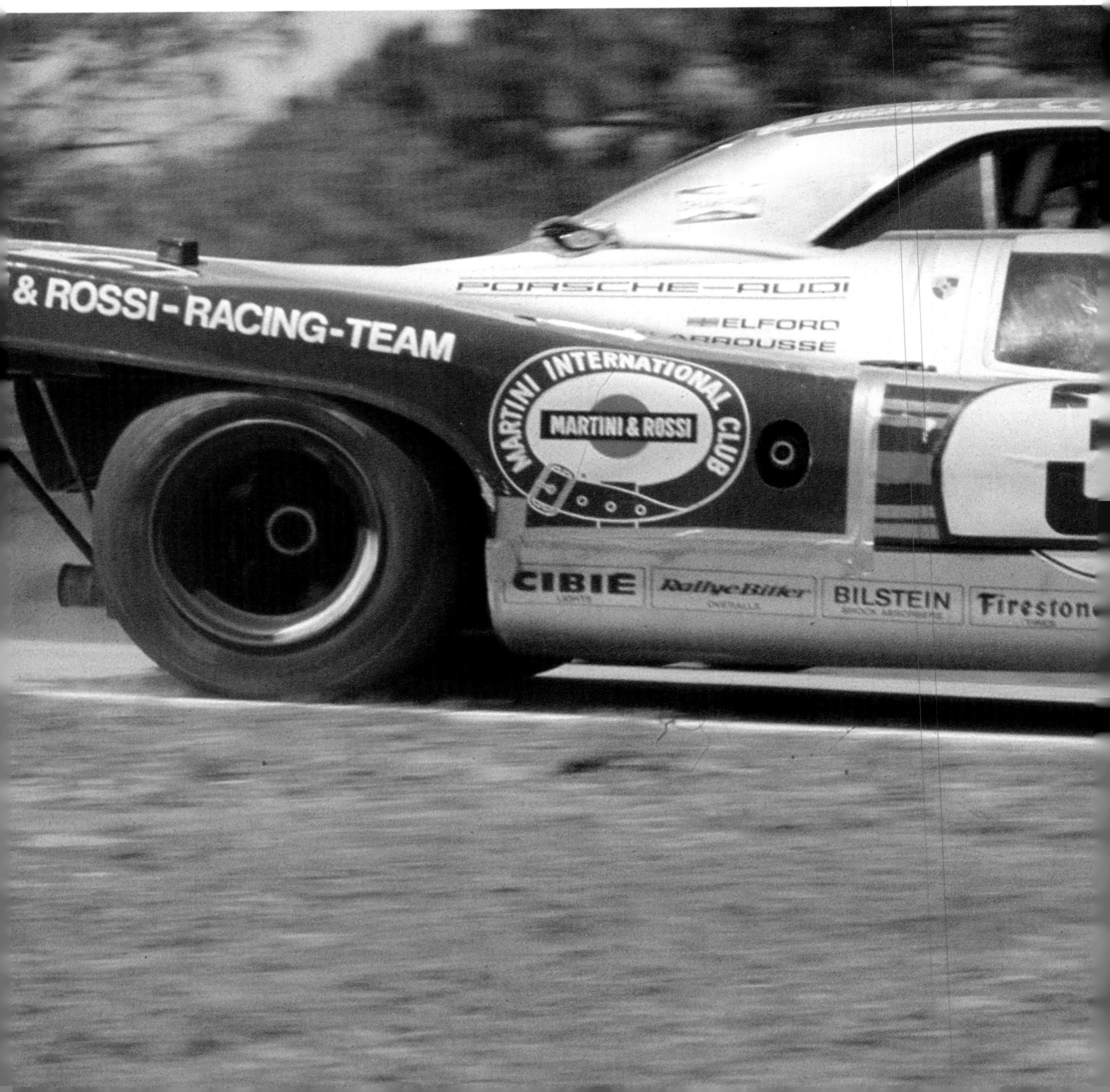
& ROSSI-RACING-TEAM
PORSCHE-AUDI
ELFORD
MARTINI INTERNATIONAL CLUB
MARTINI & ROSSI
CIBIE
BILSTEIN

TEAM AUTO

Shell
3
MARTINI & ROSSI
RACING-TEAM
Shell

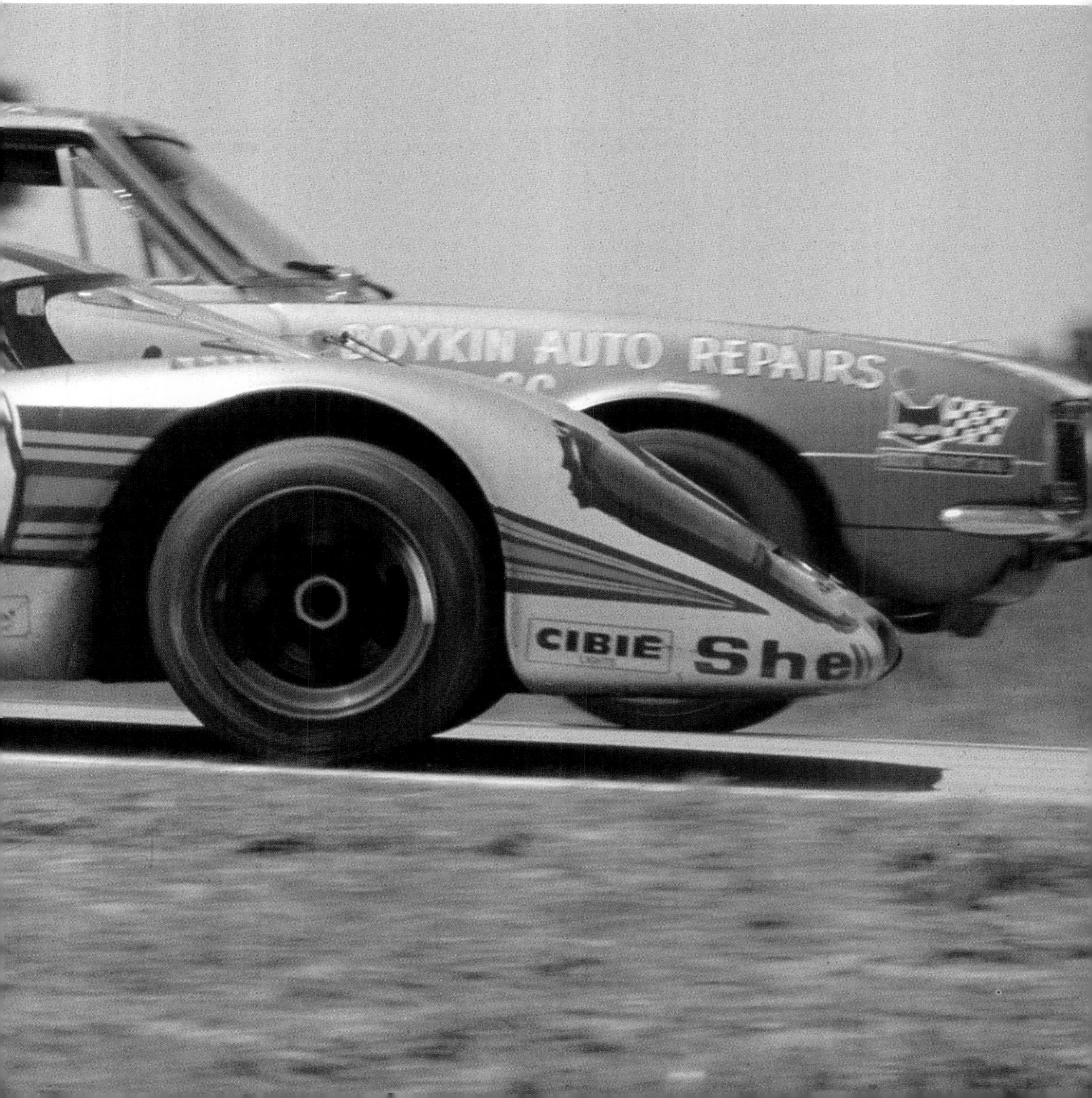

motion, and the instruction was working — the wall was gradually getting further away...''

Elford's tyre had gone, but there was no chance of limping back to the pits, the speed of rotation having taken away much of the right rear corner. In any case an errant 911 hit the car as its disorientated driver scrambled clear in the dark: ''I didn't know in which direction to run until I saw the headlights of that car coming!''

The second Martini car subsequently hit the wall due to a burst tyre after many delays, while the Penske car's catalogue of problems had included a collision with a 911. All of which left Rodriguez/Oliver 43 laps ahead after 18 hours, in spite of a split exhaust. Alas, at 11.30 am. Oliver came in with the car locked into top gear. The synchro clutch had unscrewed itself from the free running gear, blocking the gearbox. As the box couldn't be changed according to the rules, it had to be rebuilt. Ramirez: ''it took a long time to strip out. We had to resort to hammer, lever and heat...'' In all the job took 91 minutes, the car rejoining two laps behind the NART 512S that had been way behind in second place. Rodriguez had no trouble in winning by a clear lap. But this was a victory by the JWA mechanics.

The Donohue-driven Penske 512M was ver rapid at Dayto and Sebring, w it is seen here. Note the car's standard slab and full width wing.

Peter Davies refuels Siffert during the Bue Aires race. Po has yet to ado high pressure refuelling thro dry-break valv

After the race Horsman asked Porsche to put a lefthand thread on the second and fourth gear clutches so that, as with the other (righthand threaded but opposite facing) clutches, synchronizing torque would tend to tighten rather than untighten. He recalls that some concern was expressed over the number of parts that would have to be scrapped, but that the gearbox engineer ("a chap we didn't know well — he wasn't part of the racing scene") was to look into it.

At Sebring five speeds were used and the harsh braking called for caused a problem with the cross-drilled front discs, so undrilled items were substituted. Martini only had its spare car available following the Daytona shunts and this was run with a four speed 'box, but as the JWA cars with a 4.9 engine. It was driven by Elford/Larrousse. The opposition was headed by the works Ferrari 312P and the Penske 512M, with three works Alfas back in the fray.

The Maranello cars were the ones to watch as Donohue in the 512M and Andretti in the 312P slugged it out for pole. This was a five car race, the early order Donohue — Siffert — Rodriguez — Elford — Andretti. Elford was soon in trouble, clipping a backmarker while he was racing

ghi (left) and rsman (right) problem of gearbox on driguez' car. the best part of 24 hours continuous ning, bleary-eyed team rsonnel were with a total ox rebuild...

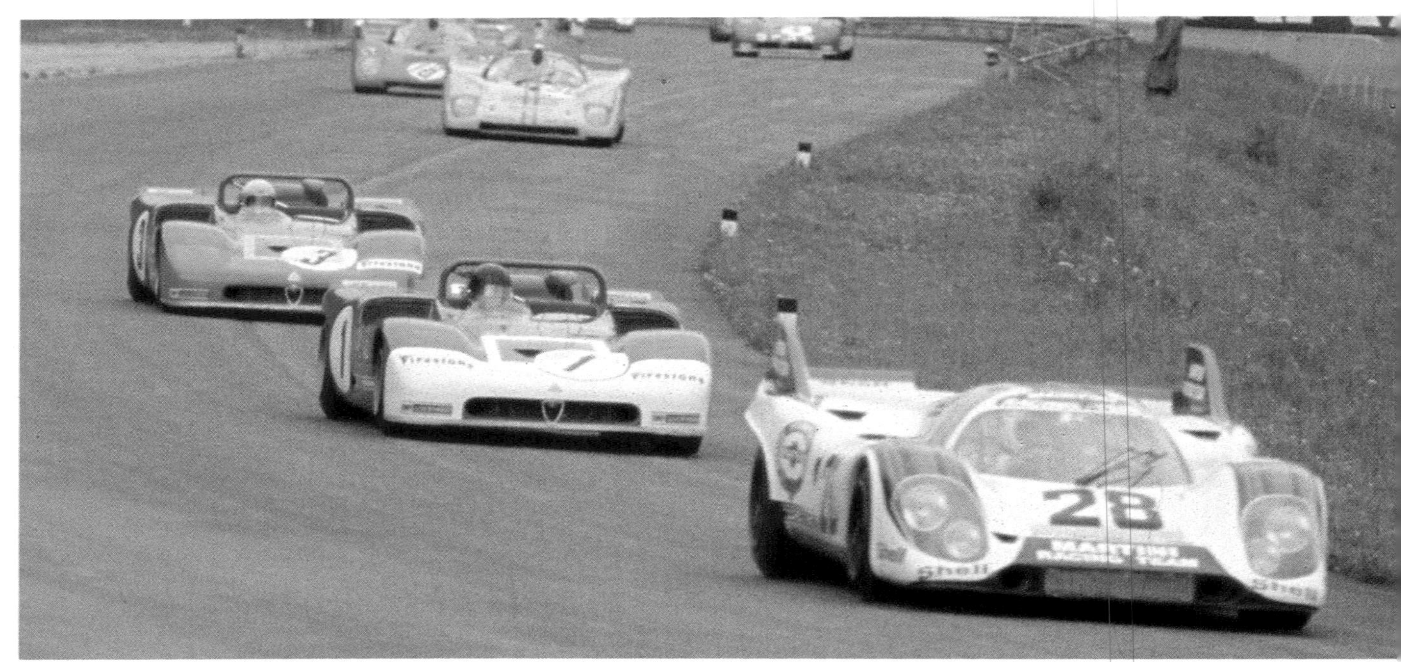

28
MARTINI RACING-TEAM
Shell
Firestone

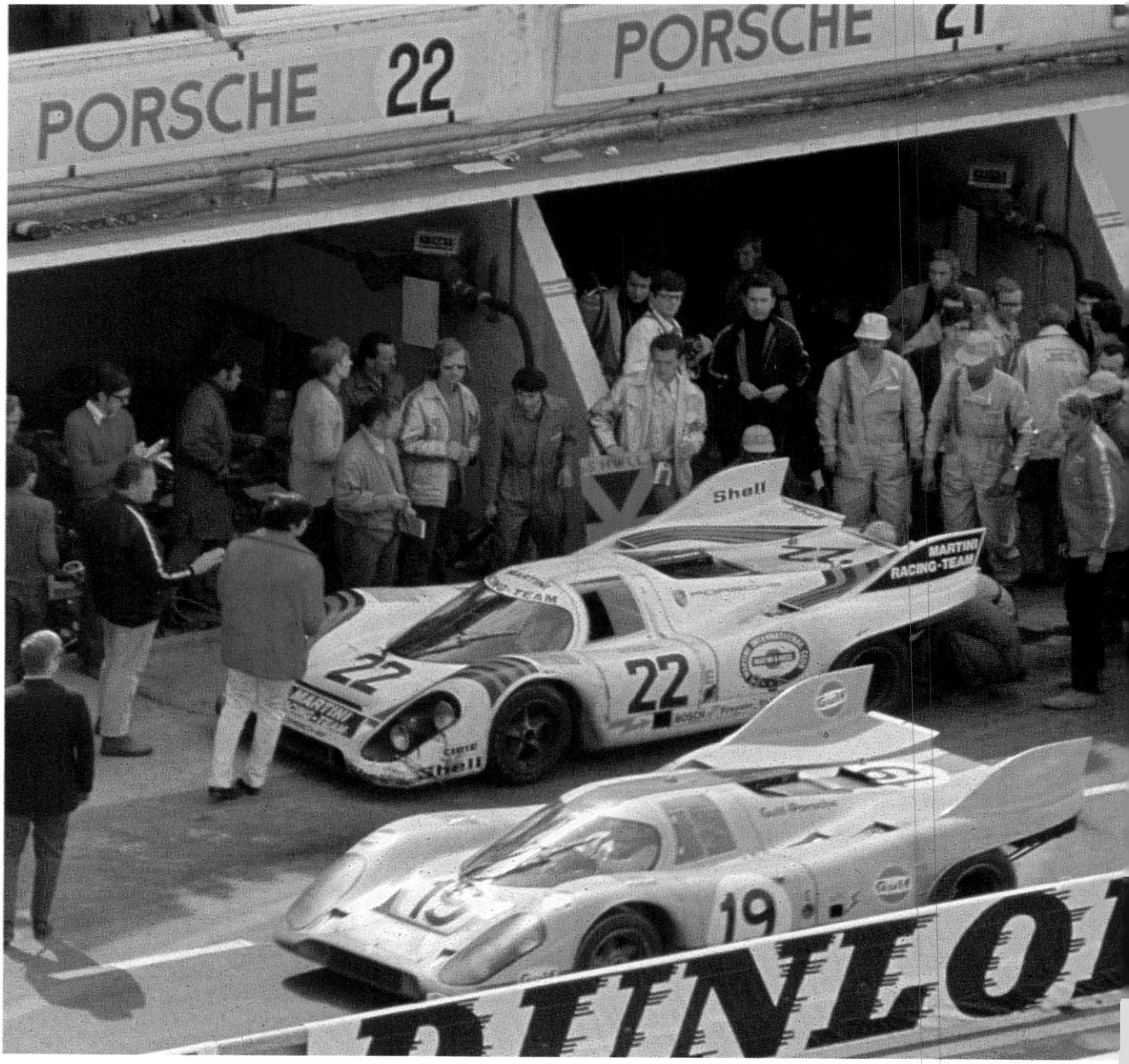
PORSCHE 22
PORSCHE 21
Shell
MARTINI RACING-TEAM
22
19
Gulf
DUNLO

maged nose
didn't harm
s chances at
, the car he
shared with
sse claiming
tory for the
artini team.
Bill Oursler

colour —
in the
team won
s, a Martini
917K of
van Lennep
ahead of
-string
try of
/Muller,
passing on
The final
rtini
were were
a 917K was

chring
hoto):
Larrouse
tyre
hile
placed.

Rodriguez. Luckily it was only cosmetic damage. When the routine pit stops took place it became clear that the 312P was considerably more fuel efficient than the Group 5 machines. That allowed it to establish itself ahead of Donohue and Rodriguez. Siffert had run out of fuel a lap before Rodriguez came in as scheduled, the car unexpectedly thirsty. Bell recalls how he and Siffert motorcycled back out to the car with Coke bottles full of fuel under their jackets! The net result was a 19 lap delay and a four lap penalty for "outside assistance".

By the three hour mark the 312P had gained a lap on Donohue and Rodriguez and looked set to win. By the four and a half hour mark Donohue had in turn got almost a lap up on Rodriguez. As he tried to pass the two cars collided. Both had to pit for repairs and with the 312P retiring a short while later due to an oil leak from the transmission cooler, Alfa Romeo unexpectedly found its cars first and second. However, Elford was steadily catching after some bother with a brake pad.

By half distance Elford was securely in the lead. With Rodriguez/Oliver losing 19 laps repairing damage to front wing and lights and replacing a broken wishbone and the 512M just as badly delayed, there was no threat to a fine win for Martini. JWA had to be content with fourth and fifth behind the Alfas, Siffert/Bell their four penalty laps behind Rodriguez/Oliver, whose car sported a headlight that the resourceful Cuoghi had borrowed from a truck!

By any analysis, Ferrari had been unlucky not to have won Sebring again. And the slick Penske refuelling had again been a revelation, though the works team had been the first to try a dry break system, at the late '70 Kyalami race. After Sebring dry break system manufacturer Avery Hardoll had a German voice on the 'phone...

For the Brands Hatch race the regulations demanded churns but Porsche was determined to introduce higher pressure. Someone had the bright idea of a gantry of five 20 litre churns feeding into a single pipe to dump the 120 litre load somewhat faster than by the traditional method. Horsman: "it was delivered to the track as a massive Meccano set and took ages to assemble on race morning — longer than anticipated. The Gulf rep wasn't there with the fuel: if we hadn't been building it we would have been out looking for him. By the time he turned up we had lost the time to flush out the second rig: the race had started. Siffert's rig was the one flushed out; it was a terrible way for Rodriguez to go out..."

Rodriguez had lasted two hours before his fuel filter had clogged, stranding him out in the country. Early on he had led Siffert but at the first stop his filler had fouled on the bodywork; this really wasn't his weekend. That had left Siffert leading, though by rights the 312P driven by Ickx and Regazzoni should have been in front. And would have been, had not Ickx fallen foul of a

PORSCHE

backmarker in the early laps. The 312P was clearly the faster car here. The JWA 917s had tried front tabs in practice and had been fitted with a splitter for the race. They also had a full 5.0 litre engine (produced simply by enlarging the bore to 86.8 mm.), all to no avail; the car wasn't well suited to the bumpy circuit (and Stommelen's Alfa as well as Ickx' Ferrari had been faster in practice).

Half distance found Siffert/Bell chased by the two works Alfas. The Alfas had always been ahead of the Martini cars of Elford/Redman (out of retirement, whereas Ahrens had gone into retirement!) and van Lennep/Larrousse. The second Martini car was running a new ram air intake. Fashioned from g.r.p., it offered a scoop for each cylinder bank, projecting above the boundary layer and having internal baffles to distribute air equally to the various trumpets. The device provided a marginal power gain at the cost of around 5% additional drag.

To its cost, Dechent's team had gambled on the wrong tyres at the start, intermediates rather than wets. And Elford had been delayed early on by a leaking tank spraying fuel onto the rear tyres. The only other Group 5 opposition was a pair of private 512s, neither of which was in the picture. And soon the Martini lead car found itself in trouble with a flash fire, fuel spilled in the undertray igniting. Redman opted to continue but Dechent quickly called him in, abandoning the effort.

Not long afterwards Siffert made a disastrous attempt to change pads: the right front wheel nut proved reluctant to come off. Previously the car had run aluminium nuts on titanium hub, here the hub was aluminium and the nut seized. In future the nuts could be surface treated. Here it cost Siffert/Bell four laps. Ramirez recalls: "the nut was going solid. Siffert was getting mad, saying 'leave it as it is and let me go', but it was neither on nor off..."

Having rejoined, the spare wheel fell out of the

Brands Hatch brought novel elling and air ection devices but there was g to spoil the f the 3.0 litre otype (right). Ferrari 312P r no. 51, seen ding Siffert's was fast but ky and victor was the Alfra Romeo of de ich/Pescarolo (car no. 54, larly pictured nd the Siffert car).

Gulf car, which was consequently blackflagged. The team had to resort to borrowing another from the Martini camp. This wasn't Siffert's day, either. Regaining ground all the time, the 312P came past to take second behind the survivor of the two car Alfa team. Van Lennep/Larrousse should have been fourth but a brake locked solid in the last half hour, dropping the car to ninth. The only private 917 in the race, that of Joest/Kauhsen, finished sixth.

This year the Le Mans test weekend didn't clash with Brands Hatch but Spanish Grand Prix commitments left Bell and Oliver to do most of the driving on behalf of JWA. Porsche had two 917Ks on hand (fitted with five speed gearboxes), a regular ex-Daytona Slough car and a white sister car from the factory. This year *Kurz* was overshadowed by *Langheck*, the revised streamliner approximately 25 m.p.h. faster on the Mulsanne, though fitting the finned tail reduced that deficit by 5 m.p.h. While the best *Kurz* time was an impressive 3′18.7″, the best *Langheck* time was a stunning 3′13.6″.

The Slough car tried ram intakes, without success. The factory *Kurz* looked normal in every respect and well used. In fact, unbeknown to its drivers, it was a brand new magnesium frame car that had only run 200 kms. The prototype magnesium frame car, 051, had suffered badly on the Weissach destruction course and this model, 052, had been built in the light of the lessons learned from it. With a frame weighing only 43 kg., the car was reckoned to carry only 766 kg (and would therefore need ballasting for a race). Due to lack of testing it was only run 15 laps, driven by both Bell and Siffert, who set the best *Kurz* time in it.

After the Le Mans test 052 was proven on the destruction course and a replacement, 053 was put in hand for the race. Meanwhile, the circus moved down to Monza where the 312P would be less of a threat. JWA had its regular entry and like Martini (Elford/Larrousse and Marko/van Lennep) opted for the finned tail which caused a little oversteer but offered beneficial top speed. Martini tried the ram air intakes again, but apart from the extra drag, fuel consumption was badly affected. Private entries came from Usdau and Zitro, while Ferrari was represented by four private 512s headed by two Filipinetti examples. Alfa Romeo pitched in with three works cars.

Refuelling was the talk of the pit lane. Porsche had constructed a vast tower, almost 10 m. high, behind the pits which allowed a tankful to gush down a 100 mm. bore pipe in less than 12 seconds (keeping within the regulation hose size and maximum pressure of 0.5 bar). The cars were sporting dry break valves and an overflow bottle was used, though Cuoghi notes that, "before you saw petrol coming out you heard a creaking and saw the g.r.p. bowing out by the side of the driver, and you were telling yourself that you were close to the maximum!". As the fuel went in with a wallop the car visibly lurched down on its springs!

The race predictably featured the three fast 917s, and as early as lap 12 the 312P and the Filipinetti 512M heading the chase were eliminated in an accident. Then Elford's car suffered a misfire, leaving JWA in charge. Soon both Martini cars were misfiring and headed for retirement. A puncture dropped Siffert/ Bell a couple of laps behind Rodriguez/Oliver but the car came through from ninth to second once more. Usdau collected seventh, Zitro ninth.

Power
5L (1971)
4·9L (1970)
4·5L (1969)
Torque
5L
4·9L
4·5L
ENGINE OUTPUT — DIN hp
400
500
600
TORQUE — m/kp
45
50
55
60
5000
7000
9000
ENGINE — rev/min

At the Le Ma
weekend a Gu
917K was run
ram air intake
a finned tail,
respectively ac
and subtractin
aerodynamic c
Only the tail
be retained fo
race.

Elford's 917 follows the ...etti 512M at ...a. In private ...'s, this year's ...re Maranello ...enge was less ...sive, in spite of a much ...nproved car.

Spa saw the same 917 cast with the 312P, a trio of 512s and one works Alfa in the hunt. Martini used the finned tail, which was worth 400 r.p.m., but JWA reverted to its regular winged tail as more downforce is needed on the sweeping curves of Spa than at Monza. In any case it was a miserable weekend for Elford: "testing once at the 'Ring I had a handling problem which turned out

to be caused by a minute crack in a front suspension mounting point. I had the same symptoms at Spa. We found a crack and repaired it but it was still undriveable. I started the race but soon packed it in — it was too dangerous".

With Elford, unbeknown to him, suffering a second minute crack of a left front suspension mounting point the race was firmly in JWA hands. In qualifying only Elford and the JWA boys had been able to get under 3′20″, Bell taking pole in the absence of Siffert and Rodriguez (due to a clashing Formula One race) in 3′16.0″ (a whisker under Rodriguez' lap record). "It was one of the most dramatic laps of my life. From Stavelot to the pits was *almost* foot to the floor all the way — I was backing off a little less each lap...exhilerating!"

From the start to the first refuelling stops Siffert and Rodriguez had been together, Rodriguez clocking 3′15.5″ to take the honour of leading. And from the first round of pit stops — with the fuel dumped from the high tower in less than 10 seconds — the cars continued to run nose to tail, Siffert now credited with 3′14.6″. The second Martini car had gone out with a fuel leak and the 312P in third place was already a lap behind.

Bell and Oliver took over for the third stints. Rodriguez had gone two laps further than Siffert on the second tankful and his car had been turned round marginally quicker, leaving Bell 23 seconds behind Oliver, which he cut to just over eight. He then gained a couple of seconds as the cars were refuelled once more and closed right up on Oliver. There was still a final late race stop, for which the co-drivers would stay put. Positions were unchanged and Yorke held out the instruction 'ROD — SIF'. Bell: "Siffert was 20 yards down the pit rail telling me to overtake. I was waiting for any error — then I would have gone by. But Oliver didn't make a mistake..."

Writing in *Motor Sport* magazine, Denis Jenkinson commented: "JW Automotive had given a truly outstanding demonstration of long distance racing with perfectly prepared cars that did not suffer from a single fault, team control and race running that was an example to all, and pit work by the mechanics that was perfection at every stop".

Won by a whisker (the cars finishing almost side by side), it had been the fastest ever road race, at an awesome average speed: 154.765 m.p.h. (not far short of Siffert's fastest lap at 161.980 m.p.h.).

Following an accident to the 312P and punctures that dropped Joest/Kauhsen to fourth and eliminated the Zitro car, Alfa Romeo collected third place. The Milan marque then went on to take a somewhat lucky win over the 908/3 on the Targa Florio. However, the Martini 908/3 of Elford/Larrousse won the 'Ring 1000 kms. Comparative tests on the re-surfaced circuit had again confirmed the suitability of the 3.0 litre car. However, Joest's 917 ran the 'Ring where constant bottoming wore a hole in its undertray. It finished a distant sixth, having had a new floor riveted in place.

Le Mans, as usual in mid June, saw six factory supported cars, all running 4.9 engines but, according to Mezger, using Nikasil cylinders for the very first time. Five speed gearboxes were standard. Of the six cars, three were factory prepared *Langhecks* for the aces (Rodriguez, Siffert and Elford), one was a unique new 917/20 while the other two were *Kurz* — a Slough prepared car and a factory prepared car, the latter 053 with its magnesium chassis.

The Slough prepared car ran the finned tail and with plain cast iron discs and JWA's usual thorough 24 hour race preparation was the heaviest 917 on the weighbridge. It was driven by Attwood/Muller. The magnesium frame car also ran the finned tail but uniquely retained cross-drilled discs and was the lightest 917, needing an extra large, 55 litre oil tank to ballast it. It was delivered white and had Martini decals added, though factory support for the back up team was stronger than ever on this occasion.

There was one other 917K in the field, the 4.5 engined Zitro car, and Group 5 was completed by nine 512s, including the Penske car, two from NART and a modified 512M from Filipinetti. The only works Group 6 entry was a single car marking the re-appearance of the Matra works team.

Clearly the *Kurz* didn't have the speed of the *Langheck* but Attwood/Muller and Marko/van Lennep ran steadily and at six hours the JWA car was the third car in a team one — two — three at the front, two laps down on the lead. Overnight both JWA *Langhecks* hit trouble but no sooner had the team *Kurz* inherited the lead than its gearbox played up: fifth gear's synchro had come unscrewed . . .

Bell admits th would have p the Siffert car the lead had made a mista the closing st of the Spa 10 km. The finis this close! Ph Gulf Archive.

Since the Daytona failure the threads had been assembled with Loctite and peened over after assembly, but Horsman's request for revised threading had fallen on stony ground. As a consequence, 37 minutes were lost. By 8.00 am. Sunday morning the car lay second, but five laps behind the Martini *Kurz*, which was the only 917 to have enjoyed a troublefree run and as a result had been leading since the 13th hour. Over the last eight hours the deficit fell to two laps, partly as a result of the magnesium car running very carefully, and having its fan changed as a precautionary measure.

The Osterreichring in late June saw only one 917 in the colours of the winning Martini team, and hastily painted at that. To be driven by Marko/Larrousse, this was another experimental factory car, having the ABS anti-lock braking system developed by Teldix (a partnership of Telefunken and Bendix) in conjunction with Mercedes Benz. In theory it made it possible to brake later into the corner. Flegl: "it worked, but

not reliably. Once in a while a wheel locked or there was a tiny delay so the driver's weren't confident of it''.

The ABS system was disconnected for the race. JWA likewise ran an experimental braking system in practice. This was a Girling twin disc system, similar to one seen earlier in the season on a Tyrrell Formula One car during practice for the Monaco Grand Prix. It had a double caliper with two pots for each disc, the discs allowed to float on the hub. Run on the spare car, it revealed snags such as sticking pistons and was put aside after practice.

The 917 line up, then, comprised three conventional 917s, each with a full 5.0 litre, Nikasil liner engine, this specification offering a healthy 630 b.h.p. which was fed through a five speed gearbox. While Martini ran the finned tail, JWA preferred the stability offered by its regular tail. The team had wider, 12", front rims under flared arches. Oliver was missing from the line up, having defected to race in the States, angering Yorke, who drafted in Attwood. The opposition included three 512s, two Alfas and the 312P, which was very competitive once more. Ickx qualified within one second of Rodriguez' pole time.

Mindful of the 917's greater thirst, Rodriguez pulled away at a couple of seconds a lap in the early stages. Then, on lap 30 of 170, he dived into the pits: it was a troublesome spark box. The car fell over two laps behind the 312P, which had the measure of the other 917s. In any case, Siffert was soon out, the clutch failing (following a poor, clutch-hurting start).

Around half distance Ickx took the 312P back from Regazzoni, the car now the best part of a lap ahead of the Martini machine, which in turn had a lap on Rodriguez. Rodriguez stopped just before the 3½ hour mark and allowed Attwood only 12 laps in his car. Thanks to those two stops he rejoined three laps down with 59 to run. Driving, in the words of Wyer, with 'a cold, implacable fury', on lap 120 he went by Ickx, onto the same lap as the Martini car. Before he had a chance to pass that it burst a tyre and spun into the guard

At Watkins G… Bell's car set fastest lap, th… coasted to a h… Note its rear scoops and refashioned n… inlet.

rail. On lap 132 the 312P made its final stop, Regazzoni taking the last stint. On lap 135 Rodriguez made his final stop, a quick fuel top up and some 30 seconds quicker than the recent Ferrari stop. He rejoined almost two laps down but, lapping faster than his pole time, was able to unlap himself on lap 147. He finished that lap 99 seconds down. With 23 laps to run, winning was just possible...

On lap 148 the 312P chassis broke, pitching Regazzoni into the guard rail. Rodriguez' uncanny stamina and sheer speed had its reward. The drive stands as an appropriate memorial to a Great Driver: two weeks later he was killed at the Norisring.

Late July at Watkins Glen saw the JWA line up as Siffert/van Lennep and Bell/Attwood, with only one other 917 in the race, Piper's car. The JWA cars would require mudflaps for the following day's Can Am race and consequently were fitted with scoops directing air onto the rear tyres. There was also a larger, square shaped cockpit cooling intake on the righthand side. Alfa Romeo entered three cars while Ferrari counted the 312P, the Penske 512M and three other 512s. Both the factory and the Penske car were stiff opposition for JWA, Donohue claiming pole and setting the early pace, while Ickx came through to second.

Early on JWA hit trouble: Siffert suffered a puncture, Bell a broken throttle cable as he was making up ground on Donohue (and just after he had set fastest lap). Bell recalls that he had to jam the throttle open on tickover with a piece of wood to be able to trickle back to the pits. He lost 15 minutes.

Siffert/van Lennep struck more punctures and a misfire when it started to rain in the late stages. With both fast Ferraris sidelined, that left Alfa Romeo its third victory of 1971. The Siffert car was second, two laps down, while the Bell car was third, ten laps down after suffering its share of punctures. The following day all three Gulf cars ran in the Can Am race, van Lennep finishing ninth, Bell 11th and Attwood 13th.

After Watkins Glen all but one of the race cars, the spare parts and the 911 road cars were returned from Slough to Stuttgart. The team had already resumed work on the Mirage project but the 917 retained was to be run in the Barcelona and Paris 1000 km. non-championship races in October, driven by Bell and van Lennep. The twisty Montjuinch Park circuit was not well suited to a Group 5 car and the local Avgas fouled the plugs, the car running on 11 cylinders for much of the way. Bell recalls that he could pass Peterson's 2.0 litre Lola on 12 cylinders, then would have to watch the little car go ahead again as his misfire returned. Later a brake pad stuck, costing five laps to the winning Lola.

Montlhery was more successful, with the same engine and a change of plugs. Bell: "the car was superb and it was very memorable to win the last race".

This twin disc system was de… by AP and wa… only run at th… Osterreichring… the spare JW… It was not rac… lacking development t…

A new image

Revised ...ck—*star of* ...*st weekend.*

Since Le Mans 1970 the effort had continued further to refine the shape of the *Langheck*, which for 1971 would run on 17″ wide rear rims in the interests of improved handling. When it reappeared at the 1971 Le Mans test weekend, chassis 043 had a revised, shorter nose (accentuating the concave form) with lower, wider oil cooler and a blunt prow wrapping around to each wheel arch opening. It had larger extractor louvres set in lowered front arches with almost side-by-side headlights dictating a wider transparent cover. The car also had a revised tail with lowered hump over the necessarily wider arches and revised fins, while on the sides of the tail the top half of each rear wheel was no longer exposed. There was only a narrow, crescent-shaped slot to feed air into the partially-faired wheel well.

The fact that relatively little suspension movement is required at Le Mans had allowed the arches to be lowered. Another innovation was the use of a transmission oil radiator to reduce drag. Now at the rear three NACA ducts replaced the scoops for transmission and brake cooling, for the former a central duct aft of the engine, for the latter a duct in the front of each wheel arch hump. The nose also had three NACA ducts, one set just above each headlight with the third just in front of

the windscreen collecting cockpit cooling air. Careful attention had also been paid to the engine cooling air outlet as the underside was still faired-in.

The modifications were reckoned to have preserved the drag co-efficient of 0.36 in spite of a slightly wider frontal area and more downforce at the front. The revised nose countered any tendency to lift while the tips of the fins were now out of the backwash from the cabin, keeping the car more stable in yaw (such as while drifting through a bend). Certainly, the result was impressive on the track, Oliver touching 240 m.p.h. and cutting a remarkable 3′13.6″ lap. He reported that the car was completely stable on the Mulsanne, and could be moved from one side of the road to the other without problem. Bell also found it stable through the kink, though after the *Kurz* he likened its handling to "having a caravan on the back".

This year JWA agreed to race the car. Horsman reflects that, "the 1970 version had been a bit dodgy, but having declined to use it we had found ourselves battling with Elford. We shouldn't have been in that position..." Again, it was a question of accepting the development or racing against it. The team had won previous 24 hour races by exploiting well proven technology. Horsman: "we were pressurized into using the long tail in 1971..."

Three examples were prepared for the race at Zuffenhausen, 042 going to Martini for Elford/Larrousse. They all had five speed gearboxes, 4.9 engines for proven reliability and external oil lines as favoured by JWA. This year Rodriguez got pole in 043, lapping in 3′13.9″, while he was officially timed at 240 m.p.h. Elford, having dominated Wednesday qualifying, was just

-iguez/Oliver's -angheck at Le -. The car was -ast but didn't -vive. Note the -r wheel spats.

a second slower. He found the revised 042 "a little bit better than in 1970, but even then it had been a superb car..."

Between qualifying and the race, extra cockpit cooling air was fed from small holes set alongside the brake intakes, under the headlights. The chance of one of the three *Langhecks* running through without serious delay and consequently winning had to be high. The first setback befell Siffert/Bell at dusk — a minor electrical problem that didn't cost too much ground. Soon afterwards Larrousse had the cooling fan fly off. The problem was apparently a bad batch of bolts. The car failed to reach the pits without overheating.

Soon into the second quarter Siffert/Bell suffered a more serious setback — the lefthand rear wheelbearing had overheated and seized. Clearly, the partial enclosure of the wheel well had taken its toll. Replacing driveshaft, upright and hub cost over an hour and a half. Prepared for the eventuality, the same task was completed in 22 minutes when the Rodriguez/Oliver car came in after 11 hours. It returned to the fray only to suffer a burst oil line. Horsman: "it was a bad line, bursting due to a weakness in the rubber. It pumped all the oil out on the way to the pits". Rodriguez had only the consolation of fastest lap, a record 3′18.7″.

Siffert/Bell were equally unlucky, a cracked crankcase leaking oil. Horsman recalls that, "Piëch had promised Siffert that he would get an engine for his Can Am car if he finished, so we were desparate to get him there, but we couldn't seal the crack". And boy, did they try...

While the *Langheck* had been by far the fastest car at Le Mans, this year its fuel consumption advantage had been marginal, and its pad wear had been twice as high as that of the *Kurz*.

No joke

"If the driver spun a *Langheck* it nearly always crashed, due to its length", Piëch recalls with a smile. The aim of the 917/20 project was to produce a shorter car with the handling of the standard 70/71 *Kurz* but a markedly better drag co-efficient. A low drag car without a caravan on the back! In effect, the car produced in collaboration with the SERA design office was a cross between the regular long and short tail cars with a compromise drag co-efficient. However, it wasn't merely a case of abbreviating the tail of the *Langheck*: the 917/20 had a new and very distinctive body, notable for generous extra width.

The extra width produced wheel arch overhang, providing for rounded arch edges, the aims being to reduce interference between the flow along the sides of the car and the air whipped around by wheel rotation, and to ease the flow from the arch. Of course the drawback of the extra width was an increase in frontal area, up from 1.570 square metres to 1.656.

The 917/20 carried a stubby version of the air dam nose developed for the 1971 *Langheck* with prominent louvres set into the front of each arch. The nose was, of course, concave. The car was slab sided and the trailing edge of each wheel arch was carefully rounded into the uncommonly flat flank. The tail left the engine exposed in conventional style and featured a short concave deck (without central valley) flanked by prominent fins. A small spoiler was set across the rear of the deck. Whereas the optional '71 fin tail for the *Kurz* was cutaway at the rear, the 917/20 reverted to a deep end panel with carefully shaped bodywork behind the rear tyres.

The 917/20 featured regular oil radiator and front brake air inlets and had three inlets for cockpit cooling: a central NACA duct ahead of the windscreen plus a hole either side of the main

nose intakes. At the rear were NACA ducts for brake and transmission cooling following the '71 *Langheck* pattern with transmission oil radiator.

The 917/20 was produced as a one-off, taking advantage of the relaxation of Group 5 homologation requirements. It arrived at the Le Mans test weekend unsorted, to be driven primarily by Kauhsen. To continue the setting-up process he contested the poorly supported Three Hour race which followed the trials, then pounded round the Weissach circuits.

The car was run in the 24 hours by the factory, under the umbrella of the Martini team. In his autobiography, Wyer notes that, "it was not offered to us", adding, however, that, "it would certainly have been refused..." Whereas it had been virgin white at the test weekend, it turned up for the race in pink with various cuts of pork

The chunky 917/20 was seen only during the 1970 Le Mans test weekend (left) and race week (right). Nevertheless, it was an important pointer to future aerodynamic development.

identified in the manner of a butcher's shop diagram. An inscription on the front read "The Truffle Pig of Zuffenhausen" This splendid decoration was the inspiration of Lapine's styling department and reflected, or perhaps influenced how others felt about the chunky looking car. For example, Cuoghi: "sometimes we were laughing (at Porsche) — the Pig car was a big laugh..."

Team Usdau drivers Kauhsen and Joest didn't find the 917/20 — dubbed "Berta-Sau" (Bertha the sow) by those close to it — to be a joke on the track. Joest drove it for the first time at the meeting and recalls, "it was well balanced and easy to drive. It was very good in the kink and you didn't feel the speed on the straight. The long tail cars were faster on the straight; we were faster in the corners. The long tail car oversteered more in the turns. We didn't lose too much on the straight by slipstreaming. The car was secure under braking whereas the long tail was a little nervous. But it was difficult to enter the pits, needing much care!"

At first the car had understeered but changing springs had made it handle very well and it clocked 3′21.0″ for seventh on the grid: a promising start for the 813 kg. machine which ran a fifth gear ratio in between those of the *Langheck* and *Kurz*. In the early stages the car ran strongly in the wake of the hot shots, until fan bolts started breaking, then the throttle linkage failed. Joest: "it happened at the chicane and I was lucky, I had sufficient speed to come into the pit". Overnight Kauhsen was taken ill and Joest had to drive the best part of five hours. "The car was so easy to drive, that was no problem. In a long tail car it would have been more difficult to keep going".

With the demise of the long tail cars, Berta the sow was set for a high placing, if she could last the second half of the race. Alas, Joest crashed at Arnage, under braking. "I pushed the pedal and the car turned right..." It spun backwards, clipping the barrier on the inside then crossing the track to come to rest on the outside of the corner. Damage at each end was relatively light but it had no lights and couldn't be coaxed back to the pits. Naturally Joest wasn't too popular when he returned in a course car. It was two years later that he got a phone call from a Mr Sutterfild in Palm Beach, California. This gentleman had bought the damaged car and had lovingly restored it. "He told me, 'I have discovered why the accident occured — the rear brakes were right to the metal!' "

Although its career ended in the early hours of Sunday morning, the 917/20 was not judged to have been a failure by those closely associated with it. Flegl: "technically, it was a success. It showed how the aerodynamics of the short tail car could have been improved. It had speed between the *Langheck* and the *Kurz* — in 1972/73 we could have expected an 'in between car'". He points out that it was a step along the route which would eventually lead to the shape of the all conquering mid Eighties 956 coupe, with intermediate length tail. Piëch confirms that the 917/20 was a "future car", citing as the ultimate developments of the 917 coupe adventure the magnesium frame and the shape of Berta the sow. "The 917/20 had stability like the JWA tail but a drag co-efficient the way Porsche wanted it".

Saturday afternoon and the Pig is on its way home. But it has a long way to go yet, and there are many pitfalls that lie in wait...

23
Shell
Shell

Seeing red

By the end of May the first 917/10 chassis was running at Weissach. It was essentially a rebodied coupe, as the 917PA had been. Mechanically, it featured the regular coupe specification (with Girling brakes and Firestone tyres) but it had a bespoke aluminium frame to which a new foam sandwich spyder body had been bonded. In fact, this was based on the 908/3 shape, with modified, concave nose for greater downforce. The nose was basically wedge shaped, while the rear deck was almost horizontal (only slightly upswept) and continued a flat upper surface back from the front wheel arches. The cockpit opening was wider than that of the PA as dictated by new Can Am regulations. The car carried a front splitter, front arch louvres, an adjustable rear spoiler and prominent fins either side of the rear deck. Fuel was again carried in two side tanks, a total of 300

The 16 cylind[...] 7.0 litre Can [...] engine only e[...] equipped a te[...] vehicle. The c[...] was a '69 Can[...] car with appropriately lengthened en[...] bay. Photos: Porsche.

Right, in col[...] *first race f[...] 917/10, in Si[...] hands an[...] Day-glo red [...] Watkins[...] CanAm. [...] (car No. [...] followed [...] Gulf 917s [...] JWA team-[...] Ahead are [...] (Che[...] McLaren), A[...] (Ferrari 71[...] Donohue (F[...]*

litres. With standard 5.0 litre 12 cylinder engine installed dry weight was 750 kgs.

Although the chassis was ready for the Can Am season, even a 5.4 litre version of the regular 12 cylinder engine currently installed wouldn't be available until late in the year. The 16 cylinder project had been shelved (with five engines built and only two run) in the light of 1500 b.h.p. flash readings from the fledgeling turbo engine on the dyno. Initially a 4.5 turbo was under development, with an unblown 5.4 litre available as a cheap option for Group 7 privateers (particularly those looking to Interseries).

The 16 cylinder project might have been put aside until such time as Porsche felt the need to develop a 16 cylinder, 7.2 litre turbo engine but one example had been dropped into the original Can Am spyder chassis, 027, out of curiosity. Having been suitably lengthened, 027's wheelbase now extended to 2570 mm. It was driven mainly by factory test drivers. However, by the autumn of 1971 the Penske team had been signed to handle the works Can Am effort and Donohue was starting regular visits to Weissach. He was given a run in the car and according to Flegl, "he said it had tremendous torque and that it was 'interesting' to drive, but he didn't like it..."

The agreement with Penske was for 1972 and heralded the end of the association with JWA, and the British team had decided not to pursue Can Am plans. Gulf had considered overtures from both JWA and Porsche Audi USA in respect of Can Am racing but had opted to confine its series presence to the all-conquering McLaren team. However, in spite of the fact that all the factory could offer for 1971 was a 5.0 litre unblown 917/10, Siffert again got together with Porsche Audi USA to earn some dollars. The Swiss worked out a deal with Hoppen and Steinemann whereby Zuffenhausen would loan him a standard 5.0 litre engined 917/10 and would supply sufficient spare parts to run the Can Am, while shipping the car both ways and finding the funds to run it were to be his own responsibilities.

According to Hoppen, the spyder loaned to Siffert, 002, wasn't completed until the week before the July 25th Watkins Glen Can Am and Six Hours doubleheader. So late was the 917-10 that it didn't arrive by plane from Germany in New York City until the Thursday. At this point Siffert had made some good contacts with Marlboro and the STP corporation's highly visible Vince Granetelli. Faced with footing most of the bills, he worked hard during those last few days prior to the Glen to engineer a sponsorship arrangement. In the end Siffert and Granetelli got together on a package that saw the white painted 917/10-002 go Day-glo red overnight.

"Before I left on Friday night", remembers Hoppen, "Siffert asked if he could put a few extra STP decals on the car as he was close to concluding an arrangement with Granetelli. Knowing the situation, I of course had no objections, and left. The next morning, with my

GOODYEAR

20
STP
PORSCHE
AUDI
STP
STP

Ferrari
GOODYEAR

boss in tow, I went looking for the car, but couldn't find it. All I could recall was that it was white, and naturally since it had changed colour during the night locating it proved difficult. In the end we found Siffert, but I had a great deal of explaining to do..."

In point of fact, Granetelli and Siffert had used contact paper to effect the transformation, the spyder being properly painted for the next Can Am stopover at Mid Ohio. Closely watching the car at the Glen were Donohue and Penske with the Penske team's engineer Don Cox. Donohue recalls in his book "The Unfair Advantage" that they weren't overly impressed. As he put it, "my immediate reaction was, if we're gonna race it why does Siffert have it? ... If nothing else it had to be the ugliest car in the world. Not only was it a patch up job of putting a stub-nosed roadster body on a coupe, it was very, very dirty. It had a big air cooled engine, an aluminium space frame and very heavy looking suspension and hubs".

While the shape of the red 917/10 was essentially that of a 908/3 with a high downforce chisel nose, back in Germany Flegl was busy trying a 71 *Langheck* nose and a full width rear wing on 001, in the quest for greater downforce. Donohue would test drive this car, and also the first 4.5 litre turbo engine, the development programme running to the end of the year. But perhaps more important than the shape of 002 was Siffert's connection with it. As in the endurance sphere, Porsche had in mind a back-up team with Siffert providing the support for the Penske operation.

Certainly the popular Swiss did little to tarnish his reputation in America as he piloted the 917/10 to third at the Glen, seconds at Mid Ohio and Road America, as well as fifth at Donnybrook (where he suffered fuel starvation problems in the closing laps, dropping him from third).

During this phase Siffert and his mechanics Ed Wyss and Hugo Schibler had worked out of Porsche racing enthusiast Art Bunker's Kansas City area shops. They subsequently moved to Richie Ginther's Los Angeles base (which had provided accommodation for the 917PA) for the Edmonton and Laguna Seca Can Ams. At Edmonton in Canada Siffert was fourth, while at Laguna Seca (where works McLaren driver Revson clinched the championship) he was fifth. Tragically that was his last appearance in America as the following weekend he was killed at Brands Hatch.

Following Siffert's fatal accident the car, the spares and the team's Chevrolet station wagon were returned to Europe. At the time of his accident the Swiss stood fourth overall in the championship, having driven consistently, if well off McLaren pace, generally finishing a couple of laps down. The McLaren enjoyed a 25% better power to weight ratio, and a sheer 100 b.h.p. power advantage after all. Most of the Can Am regulars adopted the attitude that if the STP backed 917/10 was all that Porsche had to offer, the championship would be a safe haven for American engines for some time to come. It was to be a rather expensive error of judgement.

Previous page, colour: *flat out the chisel-nose spyder: Siffert hounds Donoh[illegible] rapid Ferrari 5[illegible] during the 'Gle[illegible] Can Am.*

L&M

George Follmer
PORSCHE
+AUDI
SUNOCO

High pressure era

As we have seen, the decision to race a turbocharged Can Am car had been taken prior to the start of the 1971 season, indeed as soon as the Experimental Department had been sure that it could make a turbocharged derivative of the 917 competitive. Compared with the 7.0 litre 16 cylinder that had been developed in 1970, a 12 cylinder turbo engine offered more power, greater long term potential and an important relevance to future road car development.

Of course, at this stage turbocharging was virtually unknown outside of USAC oval racing where it had been employed to keep the traditional four cylinder Offy engine competitive against the more sophisticated Ford V8 that had come along in the mid Sixties. The pioneering work had been done by fuel injection expert Stuart Hilborn, engineer Herb Porter and Bob DeBisschop of Garrett AirResearch, a manufacturer of turbochargers for diesel engines. They had used a standard Garrett TE06 deisel turbo, running up to 100,000 r.p.m. and capable of delivering up to 1.7 bar boost pressure. However, even with the 168 cu. in. Offy block redesigned specifically for turbocharging the maximum boost considered safe was 1.2 bar, at which the classic four offered 625 b.h.p. — over 150 b.h.p. more than the 255 cu. in. engine it replaced.

The Offy boys were allowed to run on methanol which has a valuable cooling property; nevertheless, they had run into the sort of heat problems that face any turbo development, in particular problems with exhaust valves and seats. In response the switch had been made from an alloy block to an original-type iron Offy block, with improved water cooling flow. Such an engine finally won the Indy 500 in 1968, using a careful 1.1 bar boost for around 600 b.h.p. Better matching of turbo to engine had seen power steadily increase with bigger turbos and higher boost — up to 800 b.h.p. on 1.7 bar boost by 1971. However, the bigger turbo with better air flow was at the cost of engine response.

Engine response wasn't a vital consideration at Indy — the cars were driven in one gear around the entire course, which contained only long, wide radius bends and the driver could anticipate the point on the corner at which the power was needed, flooring the throttle appropriately. Road racing was a different ball game. A significant delay between pressing the throttle and the inrush of power would make a car undriveable on a sinuous course. By adding a twin turbo (one per cylinder bank) system to the existing 12 cylinder engine Porsche had unleashed over 1000 b.h.p. on the dyno, but could throttle lag be brought down to a manageable degree, and could adequate power be exploited without running into heat problems that would destroy reliability?

Inspiration came from the direction of Munich. Having won the 1968 European Touring Car Championship, BMW had got together with Swiss engineer Michael May (the pioneer of wings on racing cars) to develop a blown version of its 2.0 litre winner for the following season. With a single Eberspacher turbo, power had been lifted from 200 b.h.p. to 270 b.h.p. on 1.1 bar boost. But development time had been short and the machine had often suffered mechanical woes, in particular detonation. Nevertheless, the car won four races before turbocharging was outlawed for saloon car racing.

Porsche had started playing with its own 2.0 litre *Typ 910* engine in 1970, then switched to the 4.5 litre, similarly using Eberspacher turbos. The production of the base engine was straightforward enough: the compression ratio was reduced from 10.5 to 6.5:1 by changing the piston, and inlet valve lift and valve overlap were reduced by using an exhaust camshaft for both valves. It was then a case of producing a manifold to feed each banks' exhaust to the turbine and suitable plumbing to take the charge air from the compressor to the intakes via a pressure-balancing plenum chamber over each bank. That, in essence, was it: Porsche had a turbo engine to play with. An engine which, as we have seen, had the most efficient cooling of any air cooled unit from Zuffenhausen, and even had oil jets spraying the underside of the piston crowns.

The man charged with making this machine function as a winning Can Am engine was Valentine Schaffer, long in charge of the development of Mezger's various race engines. Again Falk had Flegl in charge of chassis development, but while Mezger and Falk still reported to Bott, Bott no longer reported to Piëch. In 1972 Porsche went public and all members of the Porsche and Piëch families, while retaining seats on the board, resigned from key management positions. Ferdinand Porsche handed overall managerial control to Ernst Fuhrmann while his nephew handed the Experimental Department to Bott.

By 1972 the Experimental Department had completed its move from Zuffenhausen to Weissach. Situated 15 miles from Stuttgart, it was significant that the R&D wing of Porsche was now physically separated from the car manufacturing plant for over the Piëch era it had grown into a massive concern, the expertise of which was available to outside clients. Racing and road car

Previous page, [illegible] colour: *Follmer replaced the injured Donohu[e] the Penske 917/10-turbo a[nd] won on his firs[t] outing at Road Atlanta. Howe[ver] here at Watkin[s] Glen he couldn['t] get to grips wit[h] the Chevrolet-McLaren work[s] cars. Note the adjustable outrigged rear wing.*

Donohue—a ifted driver/ eer destined play a major role in the ment of the charged 917 Flegl's ally.

development were only two departments within a giant organisation devoted to advanced technology. Of course, the racing programme was its flagship and the sight of a Can Am spyder had become a common one on the faster of Weissach's two road courses, now dubbed the 'Can Am' track. Of late at the wheel had been Donohue, star of Indy car racing so no stranger to the turbocharged engine.

Donohue had been Indy's Rookie of the Year in 1969 , had finished second in 1970 and had dominated the 1971 race driving Penske's as ever superbly prepared McLaren M16. Of course, Porsche had come across the combination of Donohue and Penske at Daytona in 1969, and again at Daytona, and also Sebring, Watkins Glen and even Le Mans in 1971. Always the combination had been one of its toughest rivals.

The Donohue/Penske association went back to the mid Sixties and by the end of 1971 embraced no less than four Trans Am championship wins. The relationship between the driver/engineer and his team owner was often likened to that between Clark and Chapman. The Philadelphia based Penske team revolved around Donohue and he would drive a single entry for Porsche in the 1972 Can Am Championship, engineered by Don Cox (ex-GM) for Penske and Schaffer and Flegl for Porsche and running on Goodyear tyres. A major difference between the past agreement with Wyer and the current one with Penske was that Penske, Donohue and Cox (who had been with Jim Hall on the Chaparrals while with the Chevrolet R&D operation) would officially be part of the factory development team.

Porsche was also supplying 917/10 customer cars with, initially, 5.4 litre unblown engines. Unlike the Europeans who had purchased 917 coupes, the American customers were often closely linked to the factory via Porsche Audi USA. Both Valsek Polak and Peter Gregg were major Porsche dealers, and both were heavily involved in representing the marque's on-track interests in North America through a number of arenas, including SCCA and IMSA production car racing. Porsche Audi USA would acquire as many development goodies as possible for these leading private entrants.

In addition to Can Am, Porsche would support leading Interseries entrants running 660 b.h.p., 5.4 litre unblown 917/10s. In 1971 the series had grown to seven events and had attracted entries from Chevrolet V8 powered McLaren, BRM and March cars against which three Porsche privateers had run converted coupes following the lines of the 917PA. And the overall winner of the series had been the example run by Finnish Porsche importer Antti Aarnio Witiuri, the AAW spyder driven by none other than Leo Kinnunen. For 1972 Kinnunen was promised the first 5.4 litre engine to be let out of captivity. The 917/10 with 5.0 litre engine was freely available for the new season, priced at DM325,000.

:he exploded awing of the Eberspacher urbocharger, l from diesel application.

f, in colour: opean ies races rks assisted fielded for en (no. 1) uhsen. Here 4 litre n cars are the let-Alcan

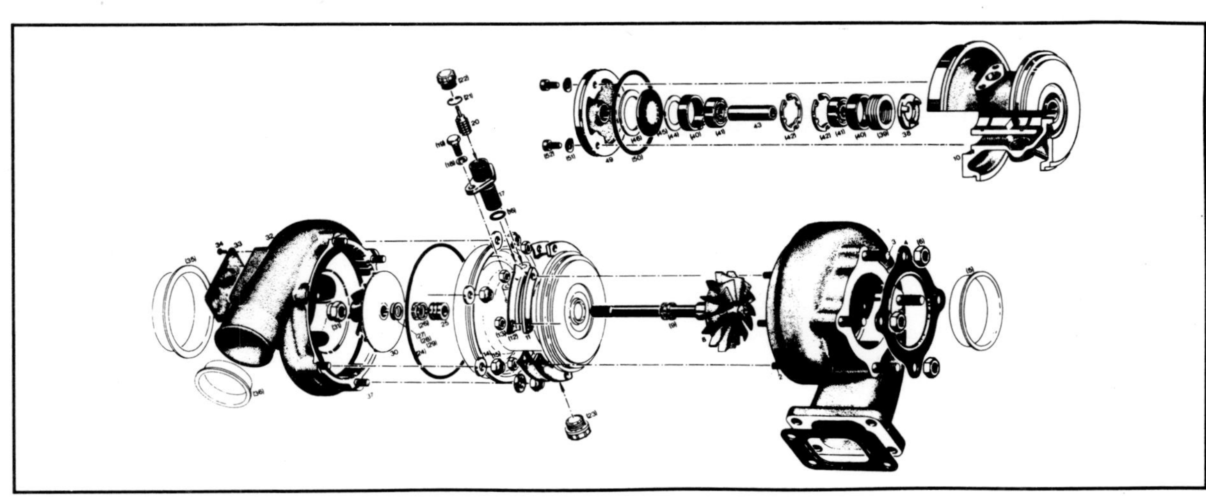

ials Formulae I and III
GO-
COLT
RACING TEAM AAW
Firestone

8
16
ALCAN

Elephant men

The nature of the Sports Car Club of America (SCCA)'s popular Canadian-American Challenge Cup series dictated the opposition Porsche found itself competing against when it embarked upon its Can Am adventure.

The Can Am was instigated in 1966 as a formalization of a loose group of races called the Fall Pro-Series which featured top European drivers handling lightweight British built, open cockpit chassis powered by American push rod, stock block V8s. The sheer strength if not sophistication of this "Detroit iron" was enough to ensure it would not be beaten by anything less than an all out effort, an effort that, at least in the beginning, wasn't about to happen. Indeed, in spite of well informed predictions that American Jim Hall and his allies at Chevrolet's R&D centre in Warren, Michigan would rule the roost, the series became the playground of Bruce McLaren, the British-based New Zealander who had started a Formula One career in the early Sixties with Cooper.

McLaren had soon launched his own company by constructing a tube-framed sports racer and by the time the Can Am was formalized he and his Oldsmobile V8 propelled McLaren M1B was a leading force in Group 7 racing. Surtees won the first Can Am in a Chevrolet-Lola T70 over Hall's innovative, high-winged Chevrolet-Chapparal 2E but when McLaren and fellow Kiwi Hulme came back in 1967 with the Chevrolet-McLaren M6 it was no contest.

Not only were McLaren and Hulme extremely talented, the 5.9 litre Chevrolet V8 powered monocoque spyders they drove were quicker by far than anything else. And the evolutionary M8 version of the simple but effective car remained in the forefront in 1968 and went on to rule the roost up until the end of 1971. The M8B, M8D and M8F were updated versions with different bodywork, the M8B introducing a strut-mounted rear wing while the M8D of 1970 started a trend of carrying the wing on rear side fences. Meanwhile the engine was increasing in displacement. From 1969 McLaren used an aluminium block version of the 427 (cubic inch) Corvette V8 and by 1971, with back door support from GM, the team's own 'McLaren Engines' facility in Detroit had reached 8.1 litres by removing cast iron cylinder liners and reducing the size of the water passages accordingly. Fuel injected, the two valve elephant engine used exclusively by the team was reckoned to produce in excess of 750 b.h.p. at 7,000 r.p.m.

The car that Porsche would face was the 8.1 litre engined M20, a straightforward evolution of the M8 series. In the case of Team McLaren the size of the operation dictated a pragmatic approach which embodied the commandment 'if it ain't broken don't fix it'. By making sure its customers always had last year's car, and by having the best engines it could find, McLaren was able to remain at the head of the field.

The M20 wasn't unveiled prior to 1972 so as not to offer any ideas to the German newcomers. At heart it was of M8 conception but detail differences added up to a new car from the pen of Formula One designer Gordon Coppuck. Thus it had a monocoque chassis cutoff at the bulkhead with heavily stressed V8 behind, supported by A-frames running to the bellhousing. The monocoque was of aluminium with magnesium floor and side sills and steel bulkheads, though the M20 deleted a front steel bulkhead. The McLaren carried fuel in traditonal side sponsons, the M20 additionally having a tank around the seats to shorten the tub. Shortening the tub allowed the engine to be pushed forward, with spacer between bellhousing and differential carrier to maintain the wheelbase. Moving the engine forward, carrying the fuel more centrally and switching from front to side mounted radiators reduced the moment of polar inertia for more responsive handling. Coppuck's switch to side mounted radiators also allowed the fitting of a wing between the front arches to cut down understeer.

Another innovation of the M20 was inboard rear brakes, McLaren using Lockheed four pot calipers front and rear. Suspension was traditional and employed magnesium uprights. The rear suspension was picked up by a yoke across a Hewland LG-MkII four speed gearbox equipped transaxle. From similar front to similar rear Goodyear tyres was further for McLaren than Porsche: 2390 mm.

Although the majority of the Can Am field was filled by McLaren-equipped privateers, Lola had not forgotton about the Can Am. After winning the inaugural series, Broadley had come back with a reworked derivative of the T70, the T160. After a relatively unsuccessful stint that had been replaced by the T220 which Revson drove for much of the 1970 season before destroying it at Road Atlanta. After that Broadley offered a lengthened wheelbase version of it, the T222 customer car, while building a one-off T260 for Stewart to drive under the L&M cigarette banner in 1971. Entered by Lola importer Carl Haas, the T260 ran the works McLarens close and even beat them at Mid Ohio. It was a direct influence upon the lower-moment-of-polar-inertia M20. However, for 1972 Lola was readying a car that was a complete departure from the T260, the T333 with pronounced wedge shape, low rear wing and servo-assisted brakes. This car was influenced by the marque's contemporary Indy contender.

The only other real opposition Porsche would face was from Don Nichols' Shadow cars, which had offered a distinctly unconventional machine with extremely small wheels. This was in the process of becoming more conventional for 1972.

nohue tried the first 917/10 plied to Penske Road Atlanta, aing a normally spirated engine. e the Langheck *nose and the adjustable rear g. Photo: Karl Ludvigsen.*

A new tune

It was the end of 1970 when Mezger's team had started work on the initial drawings for the 912 engine's turbo layout. Although Porsche had yet to discover the 912's capabilities for handling the extra heat and power it would have to endure, some definite basics had been set down that remained now, in 1972 as the turbo engine prepared to face the ultimate test. The most important of those had been the decision to use a separate turbo for each bank of cylinders. The reason for this was that two smaller turbos would "spool up" much quicker than would a single larger unit, offering better response.

The chosen Eberspacher units had characteristics not dissimilar to the Garrett turbos used in Indycar racing. Adapted likewise from a diesel engine unit, they ran up to 90,000 r.p.m. on ball bearings and delivered 0.55 kg. of charge air per second, the charge having a temperature of 150 degrees centigrade. Exhaust temperature went as high as 850 degrees and while the compressor housing and blades were of aluminium, the turbine was constructed from steel.

Along with the twin turbo layout, it had been decided to make the overall induction system as simple as possible. Log-type manifolds were used for each bank, each turbo feeding one of the simple plenum chambers and driven by its respective bank's simplified exhaust system. The two induction systems shared a common wastegate with a crossover pipe to equalize pressure on each side. The Garrett wastegate functioned exactly the way it did in Indycar racing, having a diaphragm valve controlled by an adjustable-tension set spring which allowed the valve to open once boost pressure was high enough to overcome the given tension. The idea was not to obtain the maximum possible boost, but to obtain strong boost over a workable power band.

Early dyno tests suggested that durability wasn't the best feature of the future Can Am power plant but as Schaffer continued things had gradually improved. A problem of exhaust valves tending to seize in the guide was solved by shortening the guides and modifying and chrome plating the valves. It hadn't been found necessary to alter the heads in any way and, apart from the revised, nearly flat top pistons which brought the compression ratio down to 6.5:1, the only other concessions to turbocharging were the milder intake camshaft which decreased the overlap at top dead centre and improved the engine's mid range capabilities, and a 24 mm. diameter steel output shaft.

By December of 1971 Schaffer had improved durability to the point at which one 4.5 litre unit had been able to survive an eight hour full-power run, something which reportedly could not be said for the dyno to which it was bolted. The real problems, though, weren't to be found in the dyno room — they had made themselves known on the track. Part of the difficulty Porsche faced could be traced to an engine fire in the middle of '71 in the

GOODYEAR
L&M
6
L&M
PORSCHE
+AUDI

engine cell test area at Weissach which had upset about three months development time. But, more significantly, there was still no solution to the severe lack of "driveability" which had plagued the in-car runs from the outset.

The first time anyone had faced the "driveability" issue had been when Kauhsen had buckled himself into 917/10-001 at Weissach early in the summer of '71. It had been a traumatic experience for the Porsche test driver. Flegl recalls: "Kauhsen was testing the *Langheck*, the 917/20 and the turbo engine at that time. At first the turbo took an hour or two to start! And when it eventually started it went slowly, then suddenly exploded — there was nothing in the middle. And there was long, long turbo lag — unacceptable".

Eventually, towards the end of the year, Kauhsen had been able to bring the turbo car's lap time down to 49.1 seconds, a mere two tenths faster than Donohue's best in the same car with normally aspirated engine. Siffert had also found the on-off temperament in tests both at Weissach and Hockenheim and like Kauhsen had found the engine running off after the throttle had been lifted, which caused some hairy moments. It was in the light of these experiences that a normally aspirated engine had been used for chassis development work.

Despite the fact that it hadn't been running in chassis 001, by the end of the year Schaffer had managed to mould the turbo engine's final configuration: in addition to the revised pistons and cams, cooling capacity had been increased by exchanging the bevel gears in the fan's drive so that it turned at 1.2 times engine speed and ignition timing had been fixed at 22 degrees B.T.D.C. To stop the engine running on the injectors had been positioned lower down and close to new butterfly throttle valves — fuel had been spilling even after the pump supply had been cut. The injection system was the familiar Bosch design and it required much attention during the early part of '72.

Donohue's introduction to turbocharged road racing came in late January at Road Atlanta with the latest generation 912-turbo installed in the Penske team's test spyder, 917/10-003. After towing the car to get it started, Donohue found the task of getting the car around the track to be nearly impossible due to the all-or-nothing syndrome which had plagued Kauhsen and Siffert before him. Eventually, driving on the ignition switch, an impeller failed, sending pieces into the engine, destroying it.

Another turbo-12 was supplied in March, and with it came Schaffer and Flegl. Again the venue was Road Atlanta and this time the spyder was painted in the livery of Penske's sponsor L&M cigarettes and a group of journalists had been invited to watch as part of the L&M deal's press launch. Once again, in spite of the expertise on hand, the car proved difficult to drive, sending Donohue scurrying back to Weissach with the Porsche engineers.

With Penske himself watching, Donohue struggled with 001 in turbo form, eventually recording a disappointing fastest lap of 49.7 seconds. He and Penske took the view that early Can Am events should be skipped while efforts continued to make the admittedly powerful engine more driveable. Once again a normally aspirated engine was installed in 001 while the turbo went back to the dyno. Its injection pump had now been fitted with an additional control dependent upon boost pressure.

Flegl recalls: "the breakthrough came in March, with the first Can Am round in June. With a normally aspirated car the injection system had responded to revs and throttle position — we were used to working with those parameters. Now we had a third, boost, and we had to learn how to work with this parameter. Right from the first moment the setting of the pump had been correct for high boost. Intermediate boost, low boost had been incorrect. We had to run different settings on the dyno, then all the knowledge had to be put into the injection pump. It took two or three months to produce a completely new system, with the pump about right.

"...Donohue got into the car, left the pits, put the throttle down and the engine started to run — before that he'd had something but it hadn't really corresponded to the throttle. Programming the pump properly was the breakthrough".

With everything working properly, Donohue easily took 001 around Weissach in the record time of 48.9 seconds. Other than the addition of extra valving, the engine was now ready to race. One more butterfly valve was put on each manifold, linked to the throttle and designed to bleed out air when the throttle was closed (in order to reduce the back pressure faced by the impeller in such situations). In addition, four suction operated valves were located on top of each manifold log to ensure that there wasn't a vacuum in the induction system while the turbos were spooling up.

The most significant decision at this point was to use a 5.0 litre engine as the base for the units supplied to Penske (4.5 engines being employed for Interseries use). Of the three engines sent out to Penske for the 1972 season, maximum power ranged from 894 to 918 b.h.p. according to the boost setting, which was adjusted between 1.3 and 1.4 bar. Maximum boost was attained somewhere in the region of 5,000 — 5,500 r.p.m.

Mechanically, the chassis exploiting this power was not far removed from the long distance coupes of the previous year. The departure point for the 917/10, as we have seen, had been the PA spyder of '69 — essentially a coupe with the cabin removed. In actuality, though, the first real step had been taken in the winter of 70/71 when Porsche engineers under Flegl had investigated further the rigidity of a 917 chassis. As a result of this, the frame for the prototype 917/10 had been modified to the extent of a 16% increase in torsional rigidity. Much of this had been achieved through welding 1 mm. thick steel panniers (carrying 300 litres worth of bag tanks) to the frame sills. In addition Porsche had decided to use a larger, 32 mm. diameter tube

lour:
discusses
/10-turbo
e Penske

Donohue tests t 917/10 at Weiss early in '72—sti using the Langh *type nose and v adjustable rear wing. Note that engine bay has to be enclosed.*

beneath the dash panel to decrease chassis deformations in that region.

Installation of the turbo engine had required modification of the rear pyramid frame but the consequent loss of rigidity had been regained through stronger diagonal bracing over the engine compartment. As we have seen, the original shape of the 917/10 was highly influenced by the shape of the 908/3 spyder. The car kept at Weissach (001) had been fitted with a rear wing, slung between its rear fins (apparently lack of time had prevented this development from featuring on Siffert's car).

Serious chassis development work had begun in late October (after Siffert's tragically curtailed Can Am programme) when Donohue, Cox and Penske travelled to Weissach to sign the agreement that would form the basis of the relationship between Penske and Porsche over the next three years. At this stage, Donohue found a chassis almost identical to Siffert's car, aside from the wing and a concave *Langheck*-style nose. Donohue, Cox and Flegl forged a good working relationship and took to both large and small skidpans to optimize suspension settings, spring rates and anti-roll bar sizes (building on data accumulated by Kauhsen and Flegl earlier in the year).

The Penske organisation was then sent its own, 5.4 litre unblown engined development chassis (003) and ran it at Road Atlanta just before Christmas, then at Riverside. At Road Atlanta it recorded promising times but at the faster Riverside venue it was well off the pace. Flegl recalls that while Donohue was satisfied with the chassis, he begged, "I need *more* power".

While waiting for the turbo to arrive, the Penske team made some changes to the chassis, building a new rear wing incorporating a split flap and modifying the front suspension to accept longer wishbones. The latter idea had come from Donohue's initial observation that 001 had been difficult to drive in a straight line at Weissach — "hunting all over the road" — either due to the front suspension geometry not coping with the increased front downforce, or the wider, stickier Can Am rubber.

Part of the problem was known to be that the rear roll centre was too low, a situation also causing tyre wear difficulties. But altering the front wishbones straight off reduced camber changes, helping keep the tyre's contact patch flatter to the track surface. Sure enough, at Road Atlanta in January, the revisions produced faster lap times, and Flegl and his staff went on to develop a third generation front suspension which further reduced camber change, with even longer wishbones.

Surprisingly, the rear of the chassis had been left well alone until April, when the rear roll centre had been raised by altering wishbone lengths and pick up point locations. Although the times hadn't been significantly quicker, the car had proven easier to drive and rear tyre wear had been more even.

While work on the chassis had been virtually completed by that stage, Porsche went on to improve the brakes which had shown marginal temperature capabilities in dealing with the remaining turbo lag problem (inherent in any turbo system). This was because a driver will still have his left foot on the brakes as the right accelerates early to bring the boost in as required. As a result, both the brake pad and fluid temperatures had been running much higher than the engineers would have liked, producing a spongy pedal. To compensate Porsche created its own four pot caliper brakes with special finned caliper bodies which better dissipated the heat generated and thus reduced the temperatures to more normal levels.

As the 917/10-turbo was readied for its race debut, it also sported an alternative transaxle. While the original four/five speed unit had been considered perfectly adequate for unblown engines, Flegl was worried about its ability to cope with the jump in power and torque that a turbo engine was capable of providing. This had led to the design of a much stronger four speed unit, the Type 920 (which was run with an external oil radiator). In the example supplied for Donohue the usual ZF l.s.d. had been substituted by a titanium spool to create a fully locked differential — something the Penske driver/engineer ran on all his cars.

The halfshafts were run without the ball race sliding joint, the doughnuts accounting for length variations alone. This enabled the entire shaft to be produced in titanium. The new transaxle caused the half shafts to be moved one and a quarter inches to the rear. In order to allow the 917/10 chassis to be able to accept either gearbox and have the same angularity of driveshaft, the wheelbase had been lengthened by half the shift, to 2316mm. The front track was 1620mm, rear 1586mm, while the weight was 735 kg. with a magnesium frame, as pioneered by the '71 Le Mans winning coupe.

Donohue's race car — chassis 011 — was notable for both its magnesium chassis — previous 917/10s had conventional aluminium chassis some 15 kg. heavier — and a further modified, higher downforce body which was reckoned to produce an amount of downforce equal to its own weight. Changes to the configuration Donohue had tested at Weissach in the autumn of '71 had begun with the Penske team's own wing and had led to this wing being moved back on extensions tacked on to the original rear fins. That had proved to be a more than adequate solution for obtaining proper downforce at the rear but had done little to help solve similar difficulties at the front. During testing at Riverside in January 1972 Donohue and his Penske colleagues had tried installing the front diveplanes from their McLaren M16 Indycar on the *Langheck*-type nose, with no positive results. Later a large single wing had been tried, still without any real improvement.

The factory team under Flegl took a Le Mans type nose, cut back the fenders to give them a new concave upsweep (leaving the central inlet alone) and added louvres to their front surfaces. Fences were then run either side of the central inlet and on either edge of the nose and a tier of mini wings was slung between the fences in front of the concave fender upsweep, creating what Donohue described as the ugliest nose in the entire world. Unfortunately, those winglets proved no more useful than their predecessors. However, once a lip had been added to this nose shape, less sideplates and winglets, it provided an acceptable amount of downforce.

More small modifications had come at the rear where the wheels were enclosed at the back by an extension down from the rear deck and the engine area was enclosed through two head-rest type fairings, one running back from either side of the roll bar. While neither Porsche nor Penske considered the final overall shape to be the optimum, it did its job well enough and would be standardized for all subsequent customer 917-10s.

Donohue warmed up for Mosport with some intensive testing at the Canadian circuit on the days leading up to the mid June meeting. He was clocked three seconds under the existing Formula One lap record, creating a buzz of excitement as race weekend approached. In the first qualifying session 917/10-011 set a slightly slower time but it was well clear of the field. Donohue sat out much of the second session while the works McLarens of Hulme and Revson struggled to match his time. Neither could get within a second of it, but it was clear that the new M20 badly lacked test miles...

Revson got the jump on the Porsche at the start, then the turbo boost came in... From the first corner, Donohue was in charge. But 011's advantage only held for 18 laps, then a pressure relief valve became stuck and the engine went off song. It was only diagnosed by a process of elimination and, having lost the best part of three laps Donohue was climbing dejectedly from the cockpit as the remedy was recognised. He roared back into the fray and set a new lap record before Penske slowed him down. The McLarens were cruising home with a seemingly invincible lead...

Putting a cat among the pigeons, Revson replied to news of Donohue's record with a lap 0.2 seconds faster (and close to his own qualifying time). Then, two laps from the finish, Revson's engine let go. Hulme, having dropped a lap behind due to low oil pressure and a sticking throttle, was now a target for Donohue. Another lap or so and the sick McLaren would have been caught, the Porsche finishing half a lap down, but closing fast...

Two weeks after Mosport the Penske team loaded up for some extra testing and went to Road Atlanta in North Georgia where the next round of the series was to be played out early in July. Alas, on July 3 disaster struck: an improperly secured tail section ripped off as Donohue accelerated down the main straight. The result was catastrophic as 011 flipped into the air and tore itself apart as it crashed back to earth. Although Donohue escaped from the totally wrecked car with his life, his knee was so badly damaged that it required surgical repair, putting him on the sidelines.

For Penske and Porsche things might have been worse had not the team's test car (003) been brought up to 011 specification, excepting its chassis frame which was, of course, aluminium. Interestingly, the 15 kg. heavier frame was reckoned to offer 20% greater torsional rigidity. Throughout the week leading up to the race the Penske crew toiled to turn the back up machine into the immaculate car that 011 had been before its destruction. But Donohue's intimate knowledge of the quirks of the first Porsche turbo race car couldn't be replaced.

George Follmer knew that he was under consideration as a back up driver for Penske, but hadn't expected a call so soon. Follmer was a good all-rounder who counted the 1964 US Road Racing title among his credits, and who had partnered Donohue in Penske's '67 Can Am team. Follmer was given the 'short course' in 917/10-turbo driving technique by the pain-ridden Donohue, then was sent out to uphold Porsche factory honour.

''It wasn't an easy car to drive'', Follmer recalls: ''Really, I was scared to death. I had never seen Road Atlanta, much less the Penske 917-10. It was an experience I will never forget ...''

The problem, as Follmer recalls it, involved the basic technology. ''I have driven a number of 917 coupes and they were very pleasant race cars. But, when you added the extra weight of the turbo system and all that extra horsepower to the 917 equation, it changed. It was very, very twitchy. Indeed, in fast corners you sort of 'walked' it through; letting it slide, correcting, and repeating the process over and over again until you came out the other side.

''Still, it stopped very well and, of course, it was the most powerful car I have ever driven. But, it had a short wheelbase chassis whose technology simply wasn't up to that used by the McLarens we ran against. When you added the natural problems of the short wheelbase chassis to the sudden power transition of the turbo, where you went from a low to a high horsepower situation in a real hurry, you got busy very quickly trying to keep everything under control. In fact, because of the sudden way the power came on, you really had to have the car pointed in the right direction by the time the turbo kicked in, or you could find yourself with some serious problems''.

Follmer found the Chevrolet-McLarens better sorted and was content to split them on the grid for the fast circuit as he got to grips with the new

Follmer (top) privileged to t turbo power i and generally showed the C Am regulars t business end o Penske 917/1 (right). Howe Hulme and R both enjoyed ahead of the r combination o occasion, such during the W Glen race (bel Hulme is in w McLaren no. Revson in no.

experience. He got ahead at the start but couldn't shake the orange cars off. Luckily for him, Revson stopped with a broken rotor arm on only the third lap. But Hulme kept the pressure up, drawing alongside on occasion. Then came another Road Atlanta flip, another miraculous escape, this one for Hulme. An easy win for Follmer; for Porsche, its first ever factory Can Am triumph.

Follmer went to Watkins Glen looking for more of the same and the Porsche top brass flew out from Germany to see it, along with a group of European journalists. But Follmer fumbled. While there were handling and power deficiencies, and while a valve again became stuck, Follmer never really seemed to get to grips with the car. Having lost a couple of laps in the pits, he finished an uninspired fifth. Hulme and Revson finished one — two and there were suggestions that Penske had been hasty in promising Follmer the drive for the rest of the season in the wake of the Atlanta victory euphoria. But Penske was a cool, calculating manager who knew exactly what he was doing. He sent Follmer and 003 to Mid Ohio, scene of the next race (in early August) for more testing and instigated modifications to the car.

The rear suspension was altered to accept 19″ wide rear rims and this highlighted the fact that there was little bump travel as the outside diameter of the tyres had grown with the sectional width. Raising the spring/damper mounts cured the situation and made the car easier to drive. And Porsche supplied smaller, more responsive turbocharger "snails".

Come the race and Follmer rediscovered turbocar superiority. Penske helped the cause by keeping his man out during a sudden rain storm while Hulme lost time changing from wets to dries, then back again. With Revson already out due to engine failure, Follmer marched on to his second victory. There would be no further criticism of him.

At Road America in late August the Porsche's advantage was even more pronounced. Follmer started way back in the field after commuting from the USAC Ontario 500 in California to the Wisconsin circuit and back, but quickly carved his way through to a lead he would never lose as Hulme retired with ignition failure, Revson with a broken clutch. It was now clear that if McLaren wanted to win it would have to stretch itself to breaking point, and probably beyond. The Chevrolet-McLaren was at near the limit of its potential; the Porsche had a long way to go. And McLaren had neither the time nor the money to turn to its fledgeling turbo programme.

There can have been little joy in the McLaren camp when it was learnt that the Penske organisation had taken an aluminium frame (005) and many of its spare parts to build a new chassis for Donohue to make his return to the cockpit, driving alongside Follmer. The two car act kicked off at Donnybrook in mid September, with the promise of one of the greatest races in Can Am history, each of the two opposing camps fielding its best at a track totally suited to high speed Group 7 machines. Alas, Fate decreed that all four players should drop out. The McLaren team again lacked its traditional reliability, while Donohue crashed into a field after blowing a rear tyre in the 180 m.p.h. plus first turn right hand sweeper. Then Follmer ran out of gas on the very last lap. Victory went to a year old Chevrolet-McLaren owned by Gregg Young and driven by Francois Cevert.

As a result of Donnybrook, not only was a supplementary 25 litre fuel tank fitted ahead of the right rear wheel, but since Follmer had broken an aluminium lower wishbone after hitting a kerb, these were replaced by steel items before the series headed north and west to Edmonton, Alberta with a race on October 1.

McLaren detuned its engines for greater reliability and Hulme managed second while Donohue easily won his first Can Am and Follmer, having suffered a mid race puncture, salvaged third, Revson sixth after suffering loose bodywork.

From Canada the series went west to Laguna Seca where Donohue led most of the race before allowing Follmer to assume the lead in the closing laps, a move which netted Penske's substitute driver the Can Am title. As for the McLaren boys, they had retired at mid distance while trying to keep pace with the turbocars...

Looking back over his title-winning run, Follmer reflects: "because the 917/10 had all its quirks, and because it was extremely fast (on most tracks the speeds were in the neighbourhood of 190 to 200 m.p.h.) you always had to stay on top of it. The 917/10 wasn't a docile car to drive. The steering was heavy, the throttle was heavy, and the shifting so heavy I used to get blisters on my hands from it. Even the brakes, as good as they were, required a tremendous amount of effort. It simply wasn't the most pleasant racer I have ever handled".

On the other hand, Follmer also remembers with a fondness the absolute power built into the Spyder. "It really was a car to get your attention. When I started at Road Atlanta, Denny Hulme outqualified me by a few tenths. But, by the time we got to the first turn, I was ahead. I don't think we won much because of our handling. But, we sure cleaned house with our horsepower and our braking. That was the difference".

For the season's finale at Riverside, the McLarens again went for broke, and stayed in the ballpark until the strain proved too much. Hulme parked for good, McLaren withdrawing from future Can Am participation — the series could no longer be a money spinner for the British based team. Meantime, Follmer and Donohue were heading for a one-two finish when the latter had to pit for a flat tyre — he recovered to finish third behind Revson's breathless M20.

New technology ruled supreme, and Can Am was changed for good. If that was a black mark, it wasn't against Porsche but against those who thought that good old stock block American V8s would rule the roost for ever. And if Porsche was now exploiting Can Am through technical and financial superiority, that is exactly what McLaren had done, in a more subtle way, for a number of years.

Meanwhile, over in Europe Interseries had also tasted turbo Porsche power, both Kinnunen and Kauhsen's works assisted 917/10s receiving 4.5 litre turbo motors for the latter half of the series. Kinnunen also got a Penske-style nose to replace the regular *Langheck* type and he won the series for the second year running.

73

Second Act

Having convincingly won the Can Am title in 1972, Porsche and Penske had the luxury of deciding what they wanted to do for the coming season, knowing they were in charge and not trying to catch up. It was clear that in the autumn Porsche would, as McLaren had done before it, sell its existing technology to allcomers, while developing further advances for the works team. Actually, there was little pressure on Porsche to carry development much further given that McLaren had withdrawn its opposition. Porsche, however, decided to push forward, having already begun work on 1973's 917/30 during the summer of 1972.

While the 917/30's 5.4 litre turbo engine would eventually be made available to the customer 917/10 teams, their were many improvements that Flegl and Donohue wanted to make to the works chassis to make it quicker than its predecessor. In particular, the 917/10 had suffered from a number of compromises due to the limitations of time, including the nose shape and the suspension geometry. In addition the wheelbase was relatively short, causing excessive weight transfer under acceleration and braking, with consequent adverse effects on handling. But perhaps the most significant factor was that the 917/30 was being developed in conjunction with and for one particular individual — Donohue. While it might not be the most perfect car, it should be perfectly suited to the person charged with driving it to the 1973 Can Am championship.

The 1973 turbo engine—5.4 litre and over 1000 b.h.p. at the tur of a knob.

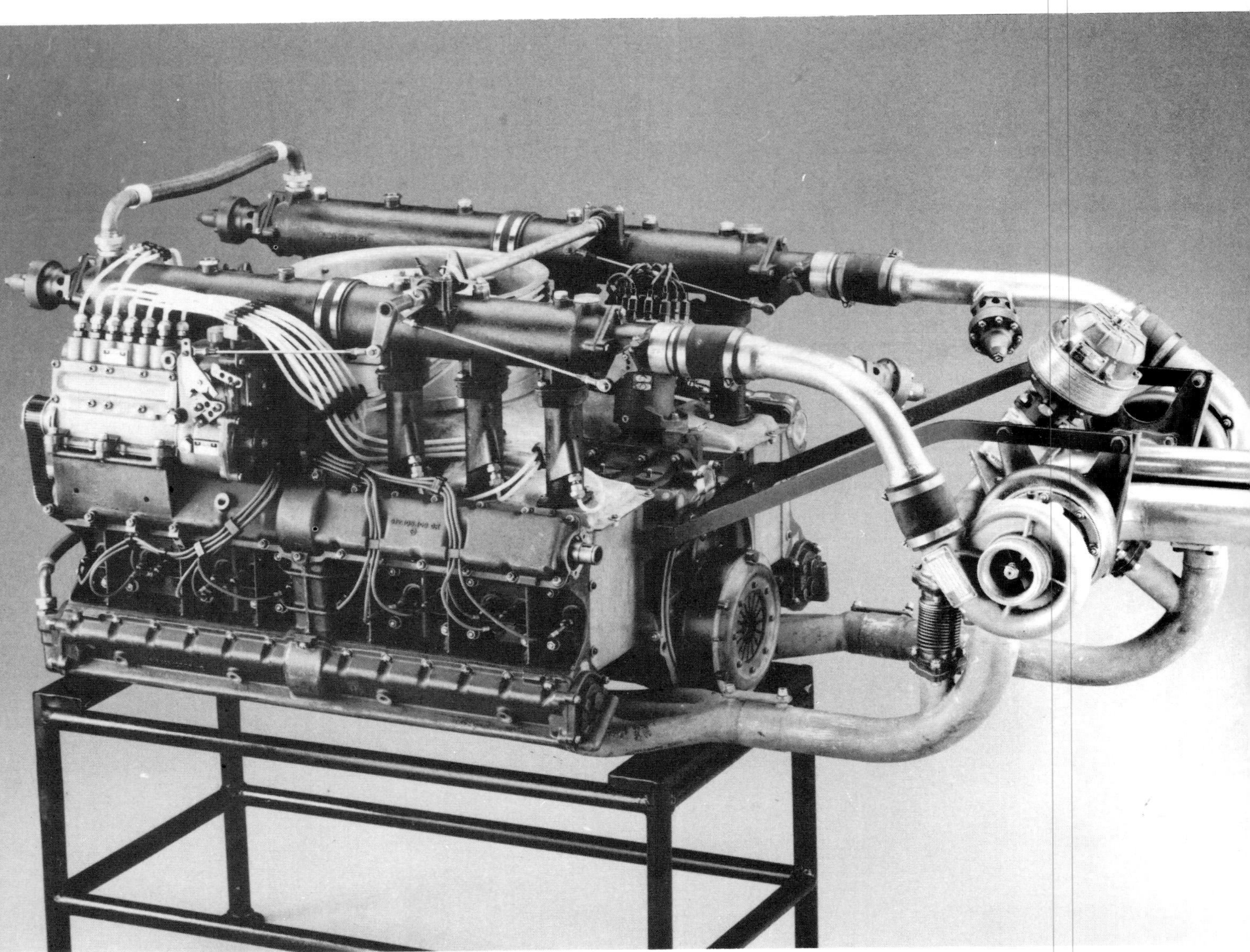

One step beyond

For those who watched the 1972 Can Am, it hardly seemed possible that there could be something beyond the Penske 917/10s. And yet, even while Follmer and Donohue were rewriting the series' tired script, Porsche was working on its definitive Can Am entry — the 917/30.

Initially little thought had been given to developing the 5.4 litre engine as part of the turbo family because its bore had been stretched to 90 mm. from the 5.0 litre's 86.8mm, considerably reducing the head/cylinder contact surface. However, by mid '72 Schaffer had started to work towards a 5.4 litre turbo for 1973 service. In so doing he created an engine which was truly awesome. With its 90 mm. bore and a 70.4 mm. stroke its actual capacity was 5374 cc. Again the cylinders were coated in Nikasil and again the compression ratio was 6.5:1. The cams remained the same but the timing was slightly altered, to 20 degrees B.T.D.C. Schaffer also simplified the induction system, eliminating the extra butterfly valves designed to reduce impeller back pressure and the suction valves, a move made possible by better matching of turbo to engine. At 1.3 bar this engine was rated at 1,100 b.h.p. at 7,800 r.p.m. and a cockpit control was provided to allow the driver to adjust the boost according to race conditions.

In spite of the engine's output, when Donohue tried it in his late season '72 chassis (917/10-005) he cut his Weissach lap time by only 0.5 second. It was clear that significant further advances would have to come from chassis developments rather than Schaffer's skills under the rear decklid. Aerodynamics and handling had both been compromised in the development of the 917/10 and both Flegl and Donohue believed these areas could be substantially improved for 1973.

Although the 917/10's body generated more than a reasonable amount of downforce, Flegl and Donohue felt that, with more power, still more downforce could and should be exploited. Additionally, Donohue's experience of the 917/10 had led him to the conclusion that weight transfer and consequent changes in handling experienced during transient phases of cornering and accelerating or braking were too abrupt. Moreover, since the Penske team had adopted 19″ wide rears the 917/10 had become especially sensitive to incorrect suspension settings in terms of handling balance. Donohue noted that if the settings were off, oversteer or understeer became particularly difficult to deal with.

Even as the Can Am was getting underway in the summer of '72 Porsche had hired Frenchman Charles Deutsch and his Paris-based SERA organisation to produce a new shape for its Can Am spyder. For the rear SERA came up with a revised wing shape that was much flatter on top and more rounded underneath. But the real change was at the front where the compromise nose was modified with the top of the fenders raised, the front lip deepened and a more angular shape overall.

To cure the balance problem, and to bring down the overall width of the 1973 entry to the slightly decreased figures demanded by the rules for the upcoming season, Porsche cut the rear track of the new car to 1565 mm. from 1640mm, while increasing the front track from 1620 mm. to 1670 mm. Track tests convinced Donohue that these changes had made the spyder an easier car to balance.

Attacking the weight transfer problem proved to be somewhat more complicated. Both Flegl and Donohue knew that they wanted a car with a longer wheelbase but neither had a clear idea of how much the chassis should be extended. Consequently, Porsche cut the chassis of 917/10 — 001 in half behind the firewall bulkhead and adapted it to take two sets of tube extensions. This allowed different wheelbase lengths to be evaluated.

In the event Donohue and the Porsche engineer settled on a 2500 mm. wheelbase having additionally evaluated 2400 mm. and 2600 mm. The extra length of the chassis allowed a substantial increase in fuel capacity, taking the total from 325 litres to 350 litres. Even so, Flegl and Mezger felt this was marginal, given the increased thirst of the 5.4 engine. Consequently they fitted additional cells to further utilize the additional space created, taking the total capacity to 400 litres, in a total of five separate bladders.

Surprisingly, the problem with the new car turned out to be its aerodynamics. In a series of tests at the Paul Ricard circuit during December Donohue and the Porsche team discovered that, in spite of all their improvements, the 917/30 wasn't any quicker in a straight line than the 5.4 litre turbo engined test machine 917/10-005. Even though Donohue dropped his times at Ricard from 1′49.2″ to 1′48.0″ with the lengthened wheelbase spyder, he was extremely disappointed that terminal speed remained as 212 m.p.h.

Subsequent discussions led to the idea of lengthening the tail portion in the manner of the *Langhecks* and this was tried by adding an aluminium sheet extension (shades of the Osterreichring test of October 1969). Donohue's speed went up to 246 m.p.h. and he decided he could live with the little loss of downforce which resulted.

Back at Weissach, Flegl adapted the rear of a 917L to the 917/30's existing deck lid, perfecting the result with reference to wind tunnel tests before shipping the first of the 917/30 race cars out to Penske in May. It was taken for testing at Road Atlanta but the exercise was cut short by a faulty weld which caused one of the lower aluminium front wishbones to break. This almost caused Donohue another flip but fortunately the incident wasn't so severe as his past Atlanta shunt and the damage to the car was relatively easy to repair. The aluminium wishbones were replaced by steel items.

Before the accident the test had shown that the long tail 917/30 was difficult to balance aerodynamically and this led Flegl to develop some right angle flaps for the rear lip of the tail. They looked good in the wind tunnel and the results were forwarded to Donohue who used the figures to create new lip spoilers which cured the 917/30's problem.

The only other difficulty experienced with the 917/30 was brake temperature, particularly with the rear discs. This was solved by the addition of a forward facing scoop to feed cooling air to the disc. Prior to this Porsche had tried reversing the cooling fan's output with negative results. In fact, the main point of making the fan suck air upwards was to win additional downforce and the concept worked fine on the dyno. Alas, in the car the vacuum created had an adverse affect on cylinder temperature and there was also a problem of the amount of dirt drawn up into the engine bay.

Come the actual Can Am season and the only question was how much better the 917/30 would be than the privately run 917/10s. This year Penske would field only one car and its developments would not be available to other teams. The car clearly handled better than the 917/10s and was of course personalized for Donohue — it was, in many ways, an extension of himself.

At Mosport, however, this singular advantage was wiped out as Donohue tagged a backmarker while running in the lead and finished outside the top five. The victor was Charlie Kemp piloting 917/10-005 under the RC Cola banner of Rinzler Racing. Kemp's triumph was largely down to general attrition as not only Donohue but also Jody Scheckter, driving Vasek Polak's new 917/10-018 very rapidly and George Follmer, who retained 917/10-003 as part of the Rinzler stable likewise failed to finish.

At Road Atlanta things didn't go that much better for the Penske team. There was a new race format with the overall mileage split between a Saturday preliminary race and a Sunday feature. Donohue won the preliminary easily (after qualifying two seconds faster than next man Follmer) but on Sunday was forced to pit with leaking fuel cap, losing almost two laps in the process. Although the 917/30 displayed its potential by allowing Donohue to unlap himself, the event went to Follmer with the Penske car runner up.

For Donohue things didn't start that well, either, at Watkins Glen which marked the third round of the series as he crashed 917/30-003 into a guard rail during practice. That, however, was the last major trauma the Penske operation would face (save for a last minute engine change at Laguna Seca). Donohue won all the remaining races. At Watkins Glen back up spyder 917/30-002 proved the equal of the regular Penske racer in all respects and somewhat luckier. Donohue won easily.

Mid Ohio was a bit more exciting as Follmer, after losing to Donohue in the Saturday race bumped his way past at the first corner on the Sunday feature. He held Donohue off until the closing stages, then the Penske driver turned the boost up and exploited the 917/30 to the full...

Over the subsequent races at Road America and Edmonton Donohue had no trouble, then came that Laguna Seca engine change. It was a temporary setback for the runaway Penske team, Donohue pulling off during the Saturday event as a broken engine stud had let the oil drain out. This led to the hurried change of powerplant and a start well back on the grid. Nevertheless, and in spite of the twisty nature of the mountaintop course, Donohue was not to be denied another triumph.

It was only on a twisty course that a 917/10 could hope to see which way the Penske car had gone, as Follmer recalls. "Running my 1972 car for the Rinzler team against Mark Donohue's 917/30 was like night and day. His Porsche was completely changed, and it really showed. On a tight course and driving as hard as I could, I could stay with him. But, at most of the Can Am tracks, such as Brainerd or Riverside, he'd just eat me for lunch".

Looking back, Follmer has some definite opinions about the influence Donohue had over the two generations of Porsche turbocar. "I think really the die was cast by the time Mark got involved in the project. There were, of course, certain things he could, and did do. But, for the most part, the parameters of the car were locked in. It was only when they got around to developing the 917-30 that he had a chance to change that".

At the Riverside finale, so great was Donohue's advantage that he was able to play with a new toy, a cockpit adjustable anti-roll bar to relieve the bordom. Having won the title, he announced his retirement from racing with the premature ending of the three-year Penske/Porsche agreement. That was in response to the SCCA's decision to severely restrict the performance of turbo cars by imposing a very stiff fuel ration. Porsche asked for the compromise of reducing engine capacity to 4.5 litres and also offered to make such an engine freely available, regardless of the chassis an entrant proposed to run. The SCCA remained resolute in its decision leaving Can Am a haven for American engines once more. But the public wasn't impressed and so few attended early 1974 races that the series had to be curtailed half way through the year.

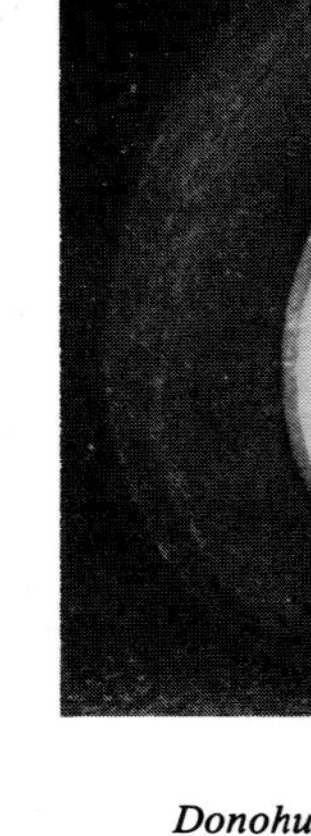

Donohu regularly front commandir Can Am from his speed office with adju boost cont deal wit hard-trying u or, more like

*him to coast
from an
ilable lead.
7/30's
ng power was
ressive as its
ver and was
d by wheel
to draw air
he brakes
).*

1969

Drivers	Chassis	Result
	Francorchamps	
Mitter	005	Rtd (M)
	Nurburging	
Piper/Gardner	004	8th
	Le Mans	
Stommelen/Ahrens	007	Rtd (Cl)
Elford/Attwood	008	Rtd (Bh)
	Osterreichring	
Siffert/Ahrens	009	1st
Redman/Attwood	010	3rd

1970

Drivers	Chassis	Result
	Daytona	
Rodriguez/Kinnunen	015	1st
Siffert/Redman	014	2nd
	Sebring	
Rodriguez/Kinnunen/Siffert	013	4th
Siffert/Redman/Kinnunen	009	Rtd(Up)
	Brands Hatch	
Rodriguez/Kinnunen	016	1st
Siffert/Redman	004	Rtd(A)
	Monza	
Rodriguez/Kinnunen	016	1st
Siffert/Redman	009	12th
	Francorchamps	
Siffert/Redman	014	1st
Rodriguez/Kinnunen	004	Rtd (G)
	Le Mans	
Larrousse/Kauhsen	043	2nd
Elford/Ahrens	042	Rtd (M)
Siffert/Redman	004	Rtd (M)
Rodriguez/Kinnunen	016	Rtd (M)
Hobbs/Hailwood	026	Rtd (A)
	Watkins Glen	
Rodriguez/Kinnunen	016	1st
Siffert/Redman	014	2nd
	Osterreichring	
Siffert/Redman	026	1st
Rodriguez/Kinnunen	016	Rtd (M)

1971

Drivers	Chassis	Result
	Buenos Aires	
Siffert/Bell	029	1st
Rodriguez/Oliver	035	2nd
	Daytona	
Rodriguez/Oliver	034	1st
Siffert/Bell	017	Rtd (M)
	Sebring	
Rodriguez/Oliver	009	4th
Siffert/Bell	031	5th
	Brands Hatch	
Siffert/Bell	029	3rd
Rodriguez/Oliver	035	Rtd (F)
	Monza	
Rodriguez/Oliver	034	1st
Siffert/Bell	017	2nd
	Francorchamps	
Rodriguez/Oliver	035	1st
Siffert/Bell	029	2nd
	Le Mans	
Van Lennep/Marko	053	1st
Attwood/Muller	031	2nd
Rodriguez/Oliver	043	Rtd (M)
Siffert/Bell	045	Rtd (G)
Elford/Larrousse	042	Rtd (M)
Joest/Kauhsen	20/001	Rtd (A)
	Osterreichring	
Rodriguez/Attwood	034	1st
Siffert/Bell	017	Rtd (Cl)
	Watkins Glen	
Siffert/van Lennep	029	2nd
Bell/Attwood	035	3rd

Can Am

The Penske Can Am campaign commenced with Donohue driving a magnesium chassis car, 10/011. After this was written off Follmer drove 003 while Donohue returned to the cockpit to drive 005. In 1973 Donohue's 917/30 was chassis number 003, with 002 as back-up—and called upon at Watkins Glen.

Key to reasons for retirement:

A	Accident	G	Gearbox
Bh	Bellhousing	M	Motor
Cl	Clutch	Up	Upright
F	Fuel system		

Note that the above list considers as 'works' cars post-69, the JWA and Penske entries plus the experimental cars — the 40 series *Langhecks,* the 50 series magnesium chassis coupes and the one-off 917/20 — regardless of entrant.

It should be appreciated that Porsche allocated a number to each spaceframe: a car rebuilt around a new frame assumed a new identity. JWA-run chassis 013, 014, 015 and 026 were re-christened in this fashion for 1971 becoming, respectively, 034, 029, 035 and 031. Further, 017 was a rebuild of 004.

JWA used 015 as T car throughout 1970, 016 throughout 1971. Each year the T car was run in the Watkins Glen Can Am (the day after the Six Hours) alongside the two race cars.

The list offered here has been gleaned from factory records.

POSTSCRIPT

professional for the 917: rands Hatch, The car is a Kremer team coupe, built with factory assistance.

Although the Penske contract finished at the end of 1973, one car was left in Philadelphia for Penske's private use. Strictly as a private entry, it was run in the 1974 Mid Ohio Can Am, this being the circuit at which Donohue had found the best fuel mileage. With the Champion in retirement Redman was invited to take the controls. The fuel metering system was modified and the boost was turned well down. And it gave the '74 pace-making 8.0 litre Chevrolet-Shadows of Oliver and Revson something to think about, Redman leading until tyre problems intervened, dropping him to second spot.

Other than that, the 917 lived on in Interseries, but in the mid Seventies the series fell into serious decline. The factory lent the original 917/30 development car, with wheelbase set as a standard 917/10 and 917/10 bodywork, to the Martini team and with 4.5 litre turbo engine Muller won the 1974 Championship, but it was a success of little prestige. The only moment of glory left for the spyder came in 1975, when Penske dusted off his 917/30 once more, this time for a closed-course lap record attempt at Talladega. With Donohue, out of retirement, at the wheel it slammed around the high-banked 2.66 mile oval and blew one engine after another as it chased the 217.854 m.p.h. record set by A.J. Foyt's Coyote Indy Car. Constant high boost running was causing detonation: the answer was supplied by Porsche in the form of intercoolers to lower the charge temperature. With an intercooled engine Donohue kept his foot down on August 9th for 221.120 m.p.h.

That would have been the end of the 917's career outside amateur and historic racing had it not been for the enthusiasm of the brothers Kremer and a timely change in World Championship prototype regulations. In the late Seventies Erwin and Manfred Kremer (well known for their exploits with silhouette Porsche 935 turbocars) started collecting 917 parts with the aim of re-creating a 917, though with no intention of racing it. By 1980 they owned sufficient parts to produce two chassis. Then regulations were published showing that a 917 would be eligible for Le Mans once more in 1981, a transitional year between Groups 5/6 and Group C...

The Kremers discussed the idea with the ACO and they liked it. So did sponsor Malardeau — Malardeau wanted a 1981 917 project. The concept was to have the attraction of racing an essentially original car, but to build it from scratch, incorporating lessons learnt from the team's emerging Group C programme.

Porsche was co-operative, clearly interested in this refresher course in coupe aerodynamics (spyders having been de rigueur for prototype racing since 1971) and supplied factory drawings and advice. The Kremer's Cologne-based 'shop also contained an ex-JWA car owned by an English historic racing enthusiast which was studied closely.

The frame was produced by the Kremers to the original design, but with some stiffening here and there as advised by the factory in the light of subsequent developments. The most difficult job was adapting the suspension to suit contemporary rubberwear, while the most interesting aspect was the team's approach to the aerodynamics of the 917K. No wind tunnel work was attempted: the result was based on the team's intuition. It featured a lowered body with nose splitter, slab sides and full width rear wing (reminiscent of the Penske 512M).

Porsche's customer service department built two engines for the project, a 4.5 and a 4.9 litre and to each was bolted a four speed Can Am transaxle. The strengthened frame with substantial roll cage bracing and the addition of air jacks was reckoned to add around 7 kg. to the overall weight. The car needed a hole in the roof to qualify for the interim 'Group 6 1981' and the Kremers were hoping that it would be more fuel efficient than the turbocars it would be running against at Le Mans.

Careful construction saw the project late for testing — it was not run until June, only getting 40 shakedown miles on the Nurburgring pits loop. In qualifying for Le Mans it was reported as lacking revs due to air starvation, but in fact the only problem was the wrong gear ratio set. Once geared as a short rather than a long tail car the strange throwback in time pulled 8,000 rather than 7,000 r.p.m. It still lacked development time, the wing making it difficult to set up. In the race it lasted seven hours, scraping into the top ten, before an 'off' while lapping a Porsche 944 ripped an oil line. Only eight litres were left when it returned to the pits, so it was withdrawn. The driver in question (who shall remain nameless here) was, in the words of Team Manager Achim Stroth, "a hasty man"...

That would have been the end of the 917's career in professional racing had the Kremer brothers not taken their 917K-81 to Brands Hatch at the end of the '81 season "to verify it was competitive". It was the last race of the interim year, the last before Group C which would usher in the 956. The race featured two serious contemporary cars, 3.3 litre 500 b.h.p. Cosworth powered 800 kg. monocoque coupes from Ford (the C100) and Lola (the T600). Exploiting the 100 b.h.p. or thereabouts power advantage provided by a full 5.0 litre engine, Wollek took the 917 around the circuit only a whisker slower than the new generation cars. He kept in touch on race day, and took a turn at leading as the others faltered. Alas, then a front wishbone pick-up broke. The 917 adventure was ended.

FROM THE PITS

USA

ROGER PENSKE

Roger Penske was the man perhaps most responsible for Porsche's success in the Can-Am. It was he who was instrumental in putting together the deals which cast the fate of Zuffenhausen's U.S. adventure into the hands of Penske's driver, Mark Donohue, and it was he who held together the team following Donohue's test crash at Road Atlanta. There Penske and Porsche were forced to create another car-and-driver combination within days, not only achieving that seemingly impossible goal, but also seeing George Follmer and the backup Penske L&M 917-10-003 win the first time out together.

Today, of course, the Porsche Can-Am years are one of many memories for the fast moving Penske, whose corporate empire is now worth hundreds of millions of dollars, and includes such things as the entire Hertz truck leasing system as well as car dealerships, race tracks, diesel engine franchises, in addition to his highly successful CART Indy Car team. Still, in spite of the years, Penske can recall clearly his association with Porsche.

"We first got together with Dr. Ferdinand Piëch at Le Mans after receiving a call from his wife. I think that happened because they were impressed with our Sunoco Ferrari 512M. I spent the next several months working out the details, including our own sponsorship with L&M. And, I believe we got along well with Porsche because they respected the fact that we didn't hold anything back; we worked as hard as we could for them to make their programme what they wanted it to be. In fact, we never really had problems with them all the time we were together.

Penske does remember also quite clearly one hurdle around which the programme's eventual outcome revolved. "There was a test session at Weissach in the spring of 1972 that I and Dr. Ernst Furhmann attended where it was obvious that while Porsche had made some progress towards improving the throttle response of the turbo engine, the gains had been relatively small.

"That night, I recall Dr. Furhmann, and I, along with several others went to dinner where we discussed the situation quite frankly. I told them there really needed to be some improvements if we were to meet our goals, and they accepted that. By the time we came back again to Weissach, they had cured the difficulties completely, and that let us go racing with confidence."

Given the outcome of the 1972 and 1973 Can-Am championship seasons, Penske's was a feeling that had not been misplaced in anyway. Penske remains less than pleased, however, with the way the SCCA decided to cripple the Porsche for 1974 because of its outstanding record. "In order to be successful in promoting a series, you have to have rules stability such as we do now in CART where I can take a year old car and win.

"For all the years that the McLaren team dominated the Can-Ams the SCCA did absolutely nothing to modify the rules. But, when we came along, and through hard work, gained a competitive advantage, they immediately moved to legislate away what we had accomplished. In light of what happened to the Can-Am after that I think they would have been much better off to have brought the rest of them up to the standard of our car, rather than to try and cut us down."

It was an era which probably won't come again. Yet, for Penske, and those who worked on the Porsche project the sense of accomplishment continues to linger on.

FROM THE PITS

EUROPE

CUOGHI & CO.

"Siffert and Rodriguez were friends out of the car but in a car, and if there was the opportunity they would fight each other. For example the Spa 1000 km. in 1971 was like a war... It has to be like that, the drivers have to feel superior and try to prove it — there was the same rivalry between the mechanics!" JWA Chief Mechanic Ermanno Cuoghi looks back fondly upon the era of 5.0 litre sports car racing, an era in which the length of a routine pit stop was determined not by a mandatory refuelling flow rate but by the skill of the mechanics.

Cuoghi was blessed with tremendous engineering intuition and bags of initiative, making him the ideal man to head the JWA spanner men. Wyer recalls in his autobiography how, when Rodriguez' car came into the pits towards the end of the 1971 Daytona 24 hours needing a complete gearbox rebuild the mechanics leapt into action, "led by the irrepressible Ermanno, completely in his element". Rodriguez' subsequent win was a classic 'mechanics' victory', and a tribute to all the lads in the JWA team.

Cuoghi worked very closely with Rodriguez and says they built up a "fantastic understanding... Pedro was tremendous with the mechanics, had good commitment and enjoyed his job so well... Kinnunen was a nice guy but I don't really think that he was ready to be driving a car like that. He was trying his best but losing too much to Pedro — that's why Pedro did most of the driving. But Pedro didn't mind. He had unbelievable stamina and the more time he was sitting in the car the better he was feeling!"

Jo Ramirez, who joined JWA for the 1971 season, was an old friend of Rodriguez, coming from the same town in Mexico. "I knew Pedro well, and I was exactly the same age as his brother Riccardo. We went to the same kart racing club and had the same racing ambitions, but they had plenty of money..." Ramirez had travelled to Maranello in 1961 with Riccardo and had started his career as a 'gofer' in the Ferrari team. Like Cuoghi, he had first moved to England to join Wyer's Slough based GT40 project in the mid Sixties but while Cuoghi had continued through the JWA project, Ramirez had gone to work for Dan Gurney in the States. When Gurney retired he had accepted an offer from Horsman to return to Slough: "Horsman didn't think it was a good idea to have two Mexicans working together so I was put on Siffert and Bell's car"

Head mechanic on the Siffert car, Ramirez recalls how Siffert "played more with the car. Pedro seemed simply to adjust himself to his car. He never seemed to be able to improve it by playing with it so he tried to adapt himself to the car!" Cuoghi recalls Siffert at the 'Glen in '71: "he wasn't happy with the car and asked to change a lot of things. Eventually we checked Pedro's car, put Siffert's on the same settings and he was perfectly happy. He was playing too much!"

At race meetings Cuoghi reported to Team Manager David Yorke — "he was very understanding with the mechanics". Peter Davies, who worked under Cuoghi, adds: "Yorke was always on the side of the mechanics. He was always out with the mechanics, and was always prepared to pay the bill. He made sure we were well fed and watered. He reckoned it was a tough job and that we should be able to enjoy ourselves".

By all accounts, JWA operated very smoothly as a fighting force under Wyer's overall control. Cuoghi says, "there was never a problem with friction in the team. Everyone had his own job, his responsibilities, and respect'. He plays great tribute to Wyer's leadership: "Mr Wyer built up so much confidence within the team from the GT40 days, we felt we couldn't fail". On the question of the Salzburg team, Cuoghi says, "we just saw a different car. We were always happy to be ahead — just like with any other team. ...Salzburg was neither friend nor foe. We were too sure of our capabilities".

Cuoghi saw the Ferrari team of 70/71 as "a different team altogether" to that which he would join in 1972. "Before Schetty and Caliri made it like an English team it was a bit chaotic". He considers the 917 was more powerful as well as more advanced in development than the 512S which was debuted at Daytona in 1970. However, the 512M that turned up at the Osterreichring was another matter. "I went to compliment Caliri, that was a fantastic car..."

The 512M run by Penske in 1971 was, according to Cuoghi, "quicker than the 917. But I didn't feel it would finish Daytona. It was too quick to last 24 hours. The Porsche was a proven package and was prepared so as to last the distance..."

Between Daytona and Sebring the JWA lads had in Gulf's Pittsburgh R&D centre what Davies describes as "two good sized bays, and excellent facilities. Anything you needed was available". Cuoghi reflects: "they had tools of any kind, and even supplied personnel to help. The cars were prepared by JWA with Gulf assistance".

Back at Banbury Avenue on the Slough Trading Estate the team had what Ramirez judges to have been "quite good facilities for those days. But we didn't have a very big machine shop and sometimes we were a little cramped — they were big cars". However, Cuoghi notes that at Slough "you could do any kind of job. And we had one of the first argon arc welders". The 917s generally arrived as a rolling chassis, though Ramirez notes that "sometimes, if there was a problem Porsche sent bits. They had more union and overtime problems than us".

The team did its own chassis and gearbox preparation, while the engines arrived packed in crates sent air cargo, ready to install. The team used the same compact four wheel truck as in the GT40 days to get to races. Ramirez: "it only had a small bench at the front for the mechanics. Mostly we had to build our own benches and work outside".

The race team working under Cuoghi in 1970 comprised Davies, Alan Hearn, Ray Jones and Richard Bray. At the end of 1970 Bray, formally with David Piper, went to South Africa and Ramirez stepped in.

The man always back at base in charge of gearbox preparation was Stan Litt. Like many of Wyer's men, Litt was an ex-Aston Martin employee. Of course, the core of the 917 team had worked on the GT40 project. Following the formulation of the agreement with Porsche, Cuoghi and his colleagues were invited down to Stuttgart, "to learn about various parts of the car. I did the chassis, the gearbox and the engine", Cuoghi recalls, "an air cooled engine was something that I didn't know anything about — it was very interesting. And we learnt how to strip and rebuild the car, how to weld it, and so forth. We were even shown an ABS system: Porsche was so advanced technically..."

Cuoghi found the 917 engine "very advanced compared with the GT40's pushrod Ford V8, but easy to work on", as was the gearbox. However, Ramirez notes that, "if the body had been detachable at the front it would have made it a lot easier to work on the chassis". Ramirez notes that the engine was a very tight fit. "You only had about 1 mm. either side as you dropped it in with the crane. Once installed, you couldn't get at some of the plugs". He says the frame was so flexible that "if you sat in the car and pushed the brake pedal very hard you could see the tubes give at the front!"

Cuoghi recalls that they never found a crack in a 917 frame. However, sometimes a frame would be found out of alignment when checked on a flat plate. If a frame took a set it could make the car unstable on the straight, "and sometimes we could correct it by moving the wishbone on the brackets with spacers", Ramirez reflects. He says that the bodywork often needed patching up and that the tubular body reinforcements were often separating. "The bodywork needed a lot of attention, all the time".

The cars were stripped down completely between races — "to the last nut and bolt", Ramirez notes — and that took, "about five days, working long hours". The cars were always immaculately turned out, JWA bothering far more about appearance than Porsche had done. Horsman was in charge of race engineering, with Falk and Flegl, "in the pit, but not interfering", Cuoghi recalls — "they were always there, in testing too, and were bringing news from Weissach".

Cuoghi found Horsman "a very logical person who didn't get over-excited and was very tolerable, but very strict at the same time". Wyer could make an expert input on the technical side but, as Davies explains, "was above the run of the mill, and more involved on the financial side. Vastly experienced, he was a very good tactician... He left the day to day running to Yorke and Horsman".

Setting up the 917K wasn't a headache as it was a well balanced car. And there were few variables to play with. There was no adjustment on the Bilstein dampers, Cuoghi recalls, and with progressive rate the springs rarely had to be changed (though harder springs were fitted for Daytona, in view of the high 'g' forces on the banking). Camber, caster and toe in were only occasionally altered; camber to suit a change of tyres, caster if the drivers complained of heavy steering. And ride height was generally standard, roll bars were left alone. In refining the car for a given track, spoiler and wing angle was the most frequent alteration: "we were adjusting spoilers quite a lot", Ramirez reflects.

Ratios were calculated in advance, by the Porsche computer and it was generally proved correct. Sometimes gearing was altered if the wind changed, sometimes for qualifying, though Ramirez says there was no real qualifying specification as such: "we just revved up the driver!"

There were no special qualifying tyres, and not many different compounds to play around with. Sometimes different rims widths were evaluated, and in the early days there was an option of a bigger tyre having a taller, softer sidewall. Fitting it meant altering the ride height and gearing to compensate. Overall though, as Cuoghi puts it "there was relatively little work for the mechanics to do!"

Sometimes engines were changed between practice and the race, and that was a task which took four to five hours, according to Ramirez. "If you didn't have an accident or an engine change it was quite relaxed, there were no long nights as a rule". Race night preparation tended to consist of the normal systems checks, plus fitting new discs, new pads, new gears and so forth, and touching up the paintwork. Then it was down to the drivers — and the speed of race day pit work with fuel and oil to put in at regular intervals, and on tighter tracks a mid race pad change. Those stops were always slick and at Spa in 71, for example, the lads helped keep the cars together with lightening pit stops as regular as clockwork.

Spa was one circuit where the senior mechanics could expect to get a drive in the car, another was Le Mans. "We were driving the cars the 40 km. by road from La Chartre to the circuit each day", Cuoghi recalls, "and we were always finding a tractor or whatever, so we had to be very careful. You could drive the 917 like a road car, the gear shift was so smooth and it was no problem to go slowly in traffic, in first or second gear, the plugs didn't get dirty..."

"It was the fastest thing I will ever drive", Ramirez grins, "going slowly you could hear a lot of small noises — it was very noisy — but go quickly and all those small noises disappeared: you could just hear the tune of the engine... The power was incredible. If you were in third gear at 60 or 70 m.p.h. and put your foot down, your head was forced back and it accelerated like a jet!"

The brakes were good, too, Ramirez says — "you put your foot hard on the pedal and it just stopped! The car was very safe to drive, but those were public roads — it was quite a responsibility. Siffert had a small accident in qualifying and didn't get a chance to bed the pads in for the race so he asked me to do a set en route. I drove fast, as hard as I could but I found the pads were hardly bedded in at all when I got to the circuit!"